Routledge Revivals

John Stuart Mill's Deliberative Landscape

First published in 2001, this book sets out to shed light on traditional controversies in Mill scholarship, underscore the significance of the contribution Mill made to associationist psychology, argue he is not entirely successful in explaining why art matters, and that this failure is linked to a deep tension in his mature work — rooted in his unwillingness to shake off the moral psychology on which he was raised. The book examines various episodes and tensions in Mill's life and work and how they relate to and inform his philosophy — while also giving a critical account of it. This book will be of interest to students of philosophy.

John Stuart Mill's Deliberative Landscape

An Essay in Moral Psychology

Candace A. Vogler

First published in 2001
by Garland Publishing, Inc.

This edition first published in 2016 by Routledge
2 Park Square, Milton Park, Abingdon, Oxon, OX14 4RN
and by Routledge
711 Third Avenue, New York, NY 10017

Routledge is an imprint of the Taylor & Francis Group, an informa business

© 2001 Candace A. Vogler

The right of Candace A. Vogler to be identified as the author of this work has been
asserted by her in accordance with sections 77 and 78 of the Copyright, Designs and
Patents Act 1988.
All rights reserved. No part of this book may be reprinted or reproduced or utilised in
any form or by any electronic, mechanical, or other means, now known or hereafter
invented, including photocopying and recording, or in any information storage or
retrieval system, without permission in writing from the publishers.

Publisher's Note
The publisher has gone to great lengths to ensure the quality of this reprint but points
out that some imperfections in the original copies may be apparent.

Disclaimer
The publisher has made every effort to trace copyright holders and welcomes
correspondence from those they have been unable to contact.

A Library of Congress record exists under LC control number: 2002280551

ISBN 13: 978-1-138-67161-4 (hbk)
ISBN 13: 978-1-315-61684-1 (ebk)

JOHN STUART MILL'S
DELIBERATIVE LANDSCAPE
An Essay in Moral Psychology

Candace A. Vogler

Garland Publishing, Inc.
New York & London / 2001

Published in 2001 by
Garland Publishing, Inc.
29 West 35th Street
New York, NY 10001

Garland is an imprint of the Taylor & Francis Group

Copyright © 2001 by Candace A. Vogler

All rights reserved. No part of this book may be reprinted or reproduced or utilized in any form or by any electronic, mechanical, or
other means, now known or hereafter invented, including photocopying and recording, or in any information storage or retrieval
system, without permission in writing from the publisher.

10 9 8 7 6 5 4 3 2 1

Library of Congress Cataloging-in-Publication Data

Cataloging-in-Publication Data is available from the Library of
Congress

ISBN 0-8153-3658-6

Printed on acid-free, 250-year-life paper.
Manufactured in the United States of America

for David and Joan

Contents

Preface and Acknowledgements	ix
Notes on Mill's Texts	xv
I. Life and Work, Men and Women, Thought and Feeling	
James, John, Harriet and Two Crises	1
Thought and Feeling	9
II. Instrumentalism	
An Obscure Doctrine	17
"Instrumentalism"	18
Instrumentalism in Contemporary Moral Philosophy	22
Connecting Contemporary Work to Earlier Work	27
Benthamite Instrumentalism	33
III. Means, Ends and Mill:	
Mill's First Moment of Crisis	41
How Mill's Crisis Embodies the Arbitrariness Problem	43
Mill's State of Mind	47
Recovery	48
The Instrumentalist and the Arbitrariness Problem	51
Tolerance and Types	56
Mill's Own Problem	59
IV. Arts and Minds	
Explanandum	61
Narrative Art and the Inferior Mind: What James Mill and Jeremy Bentham Got Right	64
Dominant Thoughts, Dominant Feelings: What Benthamite Associationism Missed	68
The New Science of Psychology	74

vii

viii Contents

Beauty and Reason	78
Whole States of Mind, Higher Pleasures	80
In Sum	84

V. Juice

Introductory Note	87
The Puzzle About Poetry	87
Habit and Nature	89
Happiness	92
The Transfer Model Versus the Magnet and Filter Model	94
The Place of Pleasure and Pain	97
Undetached Mind-Parts	100

VI.Liberty, Ideals and Moral Nature

On Liberty	103
Arguments for Individuality	105
Could the Arguments be Calculative?	108
The Argument from Ideals as a Part-Whole Argument	110
Automatons in Human Form	113
Imitation Versus Cultivation	118
Two Senses of "Character"	121
The Argument from Ideals	124
The Bifurcated Mind in the Argument from Ideals	128
Index	133

Preface and Acknowledgements

This essay began life as a doctoral dissertation about practical reason that turned on a reading of some work by John Stuart Mill. I have retained and developed the reading of John Stuart Mill, and I have kept some of the work on practical reason, but not all of it.

I intended my dissertation as a refutation of a calculative picture of practical reason (practical reason is reason in, or toward, action). Calculative pictures of practical reason nowadays get grouped together under the heading "instrumentalism." The simplest version of such a view is:

> One has a reason for A-ing only if one wants to B and takes it that A-ing is a means to, or part of B-ing, where 'A' and 'B' are intentional actions of the relevant types.

What I set out to demolish in my dissertation was a more elaborate version of the view and involved many points about beliefs and desires. Wanting to B, after all, seemed to be the source of instrumental reasons for A-ing, and, according to instrumentalism, instrumental reasons for acting are the only sorts of reasons for acting there are. Wanting to B, in turn, was usually treated as having a desire to do it (or having a desire that one do it). Taking it that A-ing was a means to, or part of, B-ing was interpreted as believing that such-and-such was the case. So it looked as though instrumentalism was a theory about two sorts of psychological states, beliefs and desires, and how, appropriately coupled, they underwrote rational action.

I thought that such a view must stand or fall on its moral psychology. I was not alone in thinking this. Instrumentalist moral psychology was a popular target for criticism among younger Anglo-North American moral philosophers in the late 1980s and early 1990s, and I think that many refutations of it were produced then. Mine was flawed by a failure to give seri-

ix

ous attention to the question why calculative pictures of practical reason seemed powerful enough to be worth attacking when instrumentalist moral psychology was excruciatingly vulnerable to criticism. It did not occur to me to wonder whether or not our real target, a calculative view of reason in action, was best interpreted as a theory about the place of beliefs and of desiderative mental states in moral psychology. In retrospect, it seems obvious to me that if a calculative view of practical reason is powerful enough to be worth attacking, then that view does not find its best expression in instrumentalist moral psychology. Instrumentalist moral psychology is easy to criticize. The view that one has a reason for A-ing only if one wants to B and takes it that A-ing is a means to, or part of B-ing, however, is not. It is entirely beyond the scope of this essay to say why the view about reasons for acting is much more powerful than the view about psychological states. But, I now think that the power of a calculative view of practical reason helps to explain the resilience of instrumentalist moral psychology.

In what follows, I have used the term "instrumentalism" to pick out a family of views in moral psychology which hold that the psychological roots of rational action set severe limitations on the role of reason in practice. I trace the fortunes of some such views through the life and work of John Stuart Mill. Mill scholars will resist the attribution of instrumentalism to him. It is more common to ascribe such views to Hobbes or Hume (although some Hume scholars reject the characterization as well). This is partly because, as I argue in the second chapter, there is precious little agreement about what's at issue in instrumentalism. (Which, in turn, I think, is partly because the strength of instrumentalism lies in a calculative picture of reasons for acting that need have no necessary link to definite positions about the metaphysics of value, about the character of belief, or about the nature of desiderative mental states, and instrumentalism is usually seen as turning on one of these sorts of views.) I hope that by the time I have discussed the cluster of views that have recently been designated "instrumentalist," and settled upon a general characterization of what they share, the description of Mill as an instrumentalist will make more sense.

Like many readers of Mill (not all of them reputable), I take it that there is a deep tension in his mature views about political and moral philosophy. I argue that this tension stems from a tension in his views about moral psychology and practical reason. Mill retains certain features of instrumentalism in the face of philosophical and personal considerations that are hard to square with instrumentalist moral psychology.

How I go about making this argument is by thinking through and

Preface and Acknowledgements xi

with Mill. The tension I trace in Mill's views derives from his struggle to make his philosophical positions answerable to his experience of himself and his world. The critical bits of John Stuart Mill's experience and thought, for my purposes, are these:

1. an unusual education at the hands of a man who had definite views about the structure of the human mind (views that embedded an instrumental vision of practical reason in a picture of the psyche as having two distinct regions, one intellectual, the other affective, which combined elements to provide volitional states);

2. a conviction that the moral psychology that informed the education was, on the whole, correct;

3. a mental crisis in which the inability to care about his own life forced him to grapple with the result of having been raised to do important intellectual work on the assumption that thought and feeling were so separated that intellect could not care about its own operations;

4. an experience of art that allowed him to begin to enjoy his own life.

In thinking through these things with Mill, I hope to shed some light on traditional controversies in Mill scholarship (e.g., on the status of the claims Mill makes about the importance of the higher pleasures, on the sense in which Mill is an anti-consequentialist utilitarian), to underscore the significance of the contribution Mill made to associationist psychology, to argue that Mill is not entirely successful in explaining why art matters, and to argue that this failure is linked to a deep tension in his mature work rooted in his unwillingness to shake off the moral psychology he was raised on. These points crop up variously in my reading of Mill. The first chapter tells a story from Mill's life (partly as a cautionary note about the status of his *Autobiography*), traces a tendency among Mill's critics to treat tensions in his mature philosophical views as a symptom of gender trouble, and links this strange critical tradition to the separation of thought and feeling that was at the core of associationist moral psychology. In the second chapter, I give an account of instrumentalism about practical reason and discuss the sense in which Benthamite moral psychology was instrumentalist. I begin my reading of Mill's first mental crisis in the third chapter. In reading the moment of crisis, I diagnose it as an emotional response to the inadequacy of the view of practical reason embodied in the relevant moral psychology. I once again draw on work by a contemporary instrumentalist moral philosopher to argue that Mill's crisis embodied a response to instrumentalism. At the conclusion of that chapter, I sketch Mill's account of how poetry brought him back from the brink of despair. In the fourth chapter, I use Mill's essays on poetry as a doorway into a discussion of the advances he made over the associationism that had informed his education, a discussion of what the higher pleasures turn out to be on the new psychology, and a discussion of the sense in which this new moral psychology makes room for anti-consequentialist utilitarianism. I take up the question about whether Mill's revised psychology works, and how we are to understand it, in chapter five. In that chapter, I argue that the remnants of the associationist separation of thought and feeling leave Mill needing to make pleasure and pain do kinds of work that they seem woefully unsuited to doing. The problem, I urge, lies in the bifurcation of the mind which remains even after Mill has supplemented his father's "mechanical" moral psychology with the suggestion that, in addition to mental mechanics, there is such a thing as mental chemistry. Finally, in the sixth chapter, I turn to *On Liberty* and trace two strands of thought about why we ought to support extensive liberty of action. I use this chapter to trace out what I take to be the central tensions in Mill's moral philosophy, and read the tensions as effects of his attempt to retain the broad outlines of instrumentalist moral psychology while adding in a new kind of mental state and a new picture of the will. It is my great hope that the essay unfolds as an interesting philosophical narrative with bearing on some controversies in Mill scholarship and on some contemporary work in moral psychology and practical reason. It is my great hope that the narrative structure will not prevent the reader from extracting arguments. There are many arguments, but I have tried to weave them together into a story about John Stuart Mill, his life, and his work.

It has been a great joy to bring together a lot of my initial work on Mill, much of which did not find its way into my dissertation and much of which I have had a chance to rethink in the course of preparing this manuscript. I am grateful to Robert Nozick for soliciting the dissertation and leaving me room to make it into a home for my work on Mill. My work on Mill has been helped tremendously by my having had opportunities to present some of the material from some chapters variously to audiences at the Scripps College Humanities Institute, and the philosophy departments

Preface and Acknowledgements   *xiii*

at the University of California at Los Angeles, the University of California at Irvine, the University of California at Berkeley, Northwestern University, the University of Arizona at Tucson, the University of Chicago, and the University of Pittsburgh. I have also been helped by students in a course I taught at the University of Chicago where we read Mill's *Autobiography* alongside *On Liberty* and *Utilitarianism*. My dissertation has floated around a bit with me, and I have been very fortunate in my interlocutors at different places. Here in Chicago, I have had the special benefit of conversation with Dan Brudney, Michael Forster, David Sussman, Kate Abramson, Jessica Spector, Lauren Tillinghast, Josef Stern, Arnold Davidson, Lauren Berlant, and Elaine Hadley. At U.C.L.A. I was greatly helped by conversations with Philippa Foot (who was retired, but came back to deliver the first Warren Quinn lecture and work with her students), Hilary Bok and Paul Hurley (who were at Pomona College and paid visits to U.C.L.A.), Kit Fine, Bob Adams, David Kaplan, Mike Otsuka, Andrew Hsu, Carol Voeller and Michael Thompson. At the University of California at Davis, I had ample opportunity to talk about practical reason and political theory with Jean Hampton, David Copp, and John Roemer. And while I was a graduate student at the University of Pittsburgh I was aided in more ways than I can mention by my teachers, my mentors and my fellow students.

In very different ways, Gayatri Spivak and Annette Baier taught me to read work in the history of philosophy carefully. Bob Brandom gave me endless support and encouragement, and John McDowell kept me hard at work in many areas with excellent criticism. David Finkelstein, Irad Kimhi, and, especially, Elijah Millgram (then a graduate student at Harvard) were my principal philosophical conversation partners among my fellow graduate students. But, perhaps above all, I owe my thanks to David Gauthier. He got me interested in ethics and practical reason to begin with. He proved a tireless opponent in argument, one who would concede a point one week, only to meet me with a fresh challenge two weeks later, and so make it necessary for me to learn many ways of supporting my views. He encouraged me to go in the directions that suited me (however odd they may have seemed at the time). In all of these ways, he was an exemplary dissertation supervisor long before I began serious work on John Stuart Mill.

I turned to Mill late in my graduate student career when many things that I had taken to be solid and settled were made suddenly unsteady by events in my life. Reading Mill became, for me, a way of figuring out how to cope with a moment of crisis by doing philosophy. My work took a quick turn in a new direction. I had no idea how even to begin to evaluate that turn in my work or my altered sense of my life. And in that moment, David and Joan Gauthier came forward and saw me through. This essay is dedicated to them, with love and gratitude.

A Note on Mill's Texts

All references to the works of John Stuart Mill in the text and footnotes of this essay are to *Collected Works of John Stuart Mill* (University of Toronto Press and Routledge and Kegan Paul: Toronto and London, 1963-1999). Citations are given in parentheses, by volume number and page number. The following list of the volumes from which I have drawn material is arranged numerically by volume number.

1.   *Autobiography and Literary Essays*. Edited, with an introduction, by John M. Robson and Jack Stillinger. 1981.

2, 3.   *Principles of Political Economy: With Some of Their Applications to Social Philosophy*. Edited, with a textual introduction, by John M. Robson. Introduction by Joseph Hamburger. 1982.

4, 5.   *Essays on Economics and Society*. Edited, with a textual introduction, by John M. Robson. Introduction by Lord Robbins. 1967.

7, 8.   *A System of Logic Ratiocinative and Inductive*. Edited, with a textual introduction, by John M. Robson. Introduction by R. F. McRae. 1973.

9.   *An Examination of Sir William Hamilton's Philosophy and of the Principal Philosophical Questions Discussed in his Writings*. Edited, with a textual introduction, by John M. Robson.

xvi   *The Deliberative Landscape*

Introduction by Alan Ryan. 1979.

10.   *Essays on Ethics, Religion and Society*. Edited, with a textual
        introduction, by John M. Robson. Introductions by F. E. L.
        Priestley and D. P. Dryer. 1969.

11.   *Essays on Philosophy and the Classics*. Edited, with a textual
        introduction, by John M. Robson. Introduction by F. E.
        Sparshott. 1978.

14.   *The Later Letters of John Stuart Mill*. Edited, with an intro-
        duction, by Francis E. Mineka and Dwight N. Lindley.
        1972.

18, 19. *Essays on Politics and Society*. Edited, with a textual intro
        duction, by John M. Robson. Introduction by Alexander
        Brady. 1977.

20.   *Essays on French History and Historians*. Edited, with a tex-
        tual introduction, by John M. Robson. Introduction by
        John C. Cairns. 1985.

24.   *Newspaper Writings*. Edited by Ann P. Robson and John M.
        Robson. Textual introductions by John M. Robson.
        Introduction by Ann P. Robson. 1986.

31.   *Miscellaneous Writings*. Edited, with an introduction, by
        John M. Robson. 1989.

9

CHAPTER 1

Life and Work, Men and Women, Thought and Feeling

JAMES, JOHN, HARRIET AND TWO CRISES

John Stuart Mill is unusual among English moral and political philosophers in the degree to which his critics and supporters have read his work as intimately connected with the circumstances of his life. By profession, a bureaucrat, by vocation, a theorist, John Stuart Mill spent most of his maturity an employee in the East India Company's London office,[1] a man jealous of his privacy who found a place public intellectual and political life in England from the 1820s until well after his death in 1873, primarily through his writings. Most philosophical commentators who discuss the relation between Mill's life and his work, however, do not focus on these things. They emphasize instead his boyhood and something of his later intimate relations. The substance of Isaiah Berlin's reading of John Stuart Mill's On Liberty, for example, begins with some facts about Mill's childhood:

---

[1] From 1828 until his promotion to Chief Examiner at the East India House in 1856, John Stuart Mill's job was to write most of the "political" letters sent from Leadenhall Street to the "governments" of the three English "presidencies" in India. "Political" correspondence was correspondence about the relations between the colonial English administrators and the Indian states and rulers. As W. T. Thornton put it in his memorial essay about Mill, "for the three-and-twenty years [prior to his becoming Chief Examiner, Mill] had immediate charge of the Political Department, and had written almost every 'political' dispatch of any importance that conveyed the instructions of the merchant princes of Leadenhall Street to their pro-consuls in Asia" ["John Stuart Mill: His Career in the India House," in *John Stuart Mill*, ed. H. R. Fox Bourne, (E. Dallow: London, 1873), p. 20].

Everyone knows the story of John Stuart Mill's extraordinary education. His father, James Mill, was the last of the great *raisonneurs* of the eighteenth century, and remained completely unaffected by the new romantic currents of the time in which he lived...He brought up his son, John Stuart, in isolation from other—less rationally educated—children; his own brothers and sisters were virtually his only companions. The boy knew Greek by the age of five, algebra and Latin by the age of nine. He was fed on a carefully distilled diet, prepared by his father, compounded of natural science and the classical literatures. No religion, no metaphysics, little poetry—nothing that Bentham had stigmatized as the accumulation of human idiocy and error—were permitted to reach him...The experiment was, in a sense, an appalling success. John Mill, by the time he reached the age of twelve, possessed the learning of an exceptionally erudite man of thirty. In his own sober, clear, literal-minded, painfully honest account of himself, he says that his emotions were starved while his mind was violently over-developed.[2]

What Isaiah Berlin called Mill's "sober, clear, literal-minded, painfully honest account of himself" is Mill's *Autobiography*.[3] The book is not inaccurate. The story of Mill's education told there, for instance, is echoed and expanded upon in several other sources. Nor is it giddy (although it gets a bit smug in the very long section devoted to the one term when he held a seat in Parliament late in his life). But, perhaps like *any* autobiography, Mill's was composed in part with an eye toward managing his reputation.

As Mill was writing the last parts of his life story, he was asked by an American journalist to send along some biographical information for an article. Mill responded:

My life contains no incidents which in any way concern the public; and with the exception of my writings, which are open to every one, there are no materials for such a biographical sketch as you contemplate. The only matter which I can furnish is a few dates. Born in London, May 20, 1806. Educated wholly by my father, James Mill, author of *History of British India*, *Analysis of the Phenomena of the Human Mind*, and other works. In 1823 received an appointment in the East India House, and rose progressively to be the head of the principal office of correspondence between the home authorities and

---

[2] Isaiah Berlin, "John Stuart Mill and the Ends of Life," Robert Waley Cohen Memorial Lecture, London, 2 December 1959, reprinted in *J. S. Mill* On Liberty *in Focus*, eds. John Gray and G. W. Smith, (Routledge: London, 1991), pp. 132-33.
[3] "John Stuart Mill and the Ends of Life," Robert Waley Cohen Memorial Lecture, London, 2 December 1959, reprinted in *J. S. Mill* On Liberty *in Focus*, eds. John Gray and G. W. Smith, (Routledge: London, 1991), p. 133.

Life and Work, Men and Women, Thought and Feeling 3

> the local government of India, a post which had been held by my
> father. Quitted the service in 1858, when the functions of the East
> India Company were transferred to the Crown. Married in 1851 to
> Harriet, daughter of Thomas Hardy Esq. of Birksgate, near
> Huddersfield and widow of John Taylor Esq. merchant of London;
> who dies in 1858. Elected to Parliament for Westminster in 1865;
> was an unsuccessful candidate for that city in 1868 (17: 1641).

Mill's brevity may have owed something to the fact that he was about to finish a long work devoted to the detail of his life, a point which he nowhere mentions in his reply to the journalist's query. It may also have had to do with the careful attention both he and the late Harriet Taylor Mill had lavished upon drafting and reworking the *Autobiography*, and his extreme reluctance to entrust anyone else with the writing of his life.[4] In its very spareness, however, the autobiographical note is in some ways as revealing as the longer work. The note implicitly links John Stuart Mill's writings to his father's, for example, and explicitly claims that John Stuart Mill's character can best be grasped by attending to his publications: Mill had come to see himself primarily as a writer. Apart from his education, apart from his intimacy with Harriet, his relations with his father and his position as principal dispatch writer in the business of India, Mill suggests, there is not much to tell about his life story.

Mill's life *was* on the whole uneventful. It was also significantly more bookish than the lives of those of his seniors with whom he surrounded himself in his youth who went straight from the debating society Mill organized when he was just sixteen into active, public careers in law or Parliament.[5] And such credit or fault as may be involved in assessing Mill's becoming and remaining an employee of East India House who wrote books and essays (rather than a lawyer-politician with a strong theoretical bent) can be laid in part at his father's and Harriet's doorsteps.

---

[4] He made special provisions for the publication of his *Autobiography* as insurance against "pretended biographies" in the February 1872 codicil to his will (31: 329). For an excellent discussion of Harriet's role in editing Mill's autobiography, see Jack Stillinger, "Who Wrote J. S. Mill's *Autobiography*?" *Victorian Studies* 27 (1983): 7-23. There is ample evidence that Harriet's editorial "assistance" substantially shaped the content and tone of the early draft of Mill's life story. His devotion to her led him to carry out the writing of the account after her death in the spirit she had urged.

[5] The relevant members of his circle were: John and Charles Austin, T. B. Macaulay, John Roebuck, Thomas Hyde and Charles Villiers, Edward Strutt, Samuel Romilly, Eyton Tooke, William Ellis and George Graham. In effect, the fate of reform in contemporary English politics was carried through the careers of these men.

4   *John Stuart Mill's Deliberative Landscape*

Just before John Stuart Mill began his apprenticeship at East India House, his father's patron, Sir John Stuart, had offered to pay his namesake's university tuition. Had John Stuart Mill gone up to Cambridge, his path into law and government would have been clear. By his mid-teens, John Stuart Mill already was reading law with a distinguished circle of (older) young men under John Austin's supervision. But James Mill refused the gift, installed his son at East India House, and set him the task of editing Jeremy Bentham's jurisprudential works instead. At Cambridge, the younger Mill would have had to subscribe to a series of religious articles, and this was a serious drawback; the boy's education had thus far been secular. But while failing to attend university put John Stuart Mill out of step with many of his closest associates, his friendships, his newspaper and journal articles, his participation in formal debates and his educational background were sufficiently strong to keep him at the thinking edge of radical and reformist politics, and to establish him as one of the most promising young philosophers of the day.

Then came Harriet Taylor, the young wife of a London merchant. She had gone to William Fox, the pastor of her church and the editor of the Unitarian *Monthly Repository*, seeking help with some philosophical troubles. Rather than undertaking to assist her himself, rather than directing her to one of the bright lights in his flock, Fox decided to that she should take her questions to John Stuart Mill. The deed was done in 1830 at a dinner party Fox arranged at the Taylors' house. At that small gathering, Mill found that he and the Taylors shared a common interest in the plight of refugees in England. But the warmth he felt for Harriet went well beyond the camaraderie afforded by affinity for a just cause. Harriet was quick-witted and incisive, busily engaged with sorting through the common run of contemporary liberal opinions, discarding some, developing others, and arguing fiercely all the while. She aspired to be a writer like another of her dinner guests, Harriet Martineau. And Harriet Taylor needed both editorial advice and someone to talk to.

Mill was perfect for the part. He had been in charge of the education of his siblings since his adolescence and was an excellent mentor. He also had recently undergone a "mental crisis" that had left him so much less dogmatic than he had been in his teens that he was in some danger of losing track of his own better judgment.[6] He had, of late, been making a study of poetry, and Harriet had, of late, been writing some. He had, of late, been widening his social circle to include people who had no direct relation to his father, Jeremy Bentham and the utilitarians. Harriet was

---

[6] The crisis and its aftermath are described in his *Autobiography* (1: 137-191).

Life and Work, Men and Women, Thought and Feeling   5

outside this sphere. He was enthralled by her. Harriet found their new friend rather grave. But this was no drawback.[7]

John and Harriet were in love within a year of their meeting, and the pressure of their affection was sufficiently unendurable to send them scurrying off to announce their situation to their respective families and intimates shortly thereafter. From the point of view of John's father and friends, the matter was a catastrophe in the making. Divorce was in those days an ecclesiastical remedy, granted solely on the grounds of adultery or brutality (John Taylor was a kind and loving husband, neither Harriet nor Mill could bear to enter into a strictly adulterous betrayal of him). Permission to remarry after divorce required an Act of Parliament. And even if Taylor had sought divorce (which he was loath to do) and even if Parliament gave Mill and Harriet permission to marry afterwards (which was wildly improbable), Harriet's three small children would remain with their father and Mill's future might be entirely wrecked by the scandal. Mill had neither the will nor the self-assurance required to brazen it out as the voice of reason in morals, law, and politics under the cloud of public disapproval that would inevitably descend if he set up house *illicitly* with Harriet. He scarcely maintained equanimity in the face of his own family's indictment of the intimacy (James told his son that open longing for Harriet constituted a reprehensible interference with Taylor's property rights in her). And while Harriet chided John for his fear of a bad publicity initially, she came to feel protective of his reputation as well. Given the

---

[7] Michael St. John Packe's description of her view of Mill is condescending, but otherwise apt:

> She preferred serious men; they were less likely to treat her roguishly, and that was her especial horror. John Mill was known as a profound philosopher, and to have him, as at first he was, for a close friend of the family, would lend ton to her household. Moreover, to talk to him freely and at length was of itself the best part of her education: for her method of assimilation was by discussion rather than by reading, and until now she had never had anyone much to talk to save [her friend Eliza Flower], who was too fanciful, and her own husband, who was too mundane. Mill's expansion into many-sidedness had made him attractive to confide in. His knowledge was immense, and he never thought any opinion absurd. Where he could add to her thoughts from his experience, he did; and where he could not, he listened respectfully to what she told him. His fault, in fact, was to be over-tolerant at this stage...Now Harriet was a good antidote for over-tolerance...It became her mission to rescue Mill from his fatuous amiability [*The Life of John Stuart Mill*, (The Macmillan Company: New York, 1954), pp. 130-31].

6 *John Stuart Mill's Deliberative Landscape*

situation of women, her own best hope for having some influence on contemporary English opinion and politics was through Mill, and, then, she had her children to consider.

Unable to find any acceptable solution to their difficulties, John Stuart Mill gradually retired from his circle. He and Harriet spent as much time as they could in each other's company, and supplemented their semi-weekly visits with a feverish correspondence. Harriet gave up her ambition to be a writer in her own right and concentrated instead on advising and supporting Mill's work. Mill was determined to serve in part as her mouthpiece.

I mention the story of John, James and Harriet in part because John Stuart Mill (understandably) neglected to mention two important life-events in his response to the American journalist. The first of these was the mental crisis he had shortly before meeting Harriet. It is treated at length in the *Autobiography*. The second, also a mental crisis, appears to have been carefully suppressed in that essay.[8] The first crisis was crucial in changing the direction of Mill's life and thought, and has been the subject of considerable scholarly and critical interest for many years. I will treat it at some length, giving still more attention to one of the most-discussed psychological episodes in the history of modern philosophy. Before doing so, however, it is well to remember that the account of the crisis and its aftermath in the *Autobiography* was carefully staged.

For example, the first mental crisis nearly coincided with John Stuart Mill's promotion from apprentice to paid staff member at East India House in 1826. The chapter of the *Autobiography* devoted to the crisis omits to link the event to this change in circumstance. What Mill has to say about his job is said in an earlier chapter. Here is the bulk of it:

> In May 1823, my professional occupation and status for the next thirty-five years of my life, were decided by my father's obtaining for me an appointment from the East India Company, in the Office of the Examiner of India Correspondence, immediately under himself. I was appointed in the usual manner, at the bottom of a list of clerks, to rise, at least in the first instance, by seniority; but with the understanding, that I should be employed from the beginning in preparing drafts of despatches, and be thus trained up as a successor to those

---

[8] For a fascinating discussion of the second crisis and its absence from the *Autobiography*, see Janice Carlisle, *John Stuart Mill and the Writing of Character*, (University of Georgia Press: Athens, Georgia, 1991), pp. 91-97.
Carlisle gives what I take to be the best psychological reading of both of Mill's mental crises. She treats both as principally vocational crises, rather than troubled moments in a badly configured, quasi-Freudian family romance.

Life and Work, Men and Women, Thought and Feeling   7

who then filled the higher departments of the office...I soon became
well acquainted with the business, and by my father's instructions
and the general growth of my powers, I was in a few years qualified
to be, and practically was, the chief conductor of the correspondence
with India in one of the leading departments, that of the Native
States. This continued to be my official duty until I was appointed
Examiner...(1: 83, 85).

At the time of the crisis, long ambitious for Parliamentary service and a
legal career, once hopeful for a chance to go up to university with his new
friends, and ready for a measure of independence, John Stuart Mill suddenly found himself established at East India House and felt himself des-
tined to a long career of bureaucratic service, continuing to live under his
father's roof and spending the whole of the days' labors under the censori-
ous paternal eye as well. Janice Carlisle remarks:

In four bloodless sentences, Mill offers the entire course of his professional career, looking ahead here as he rarely does elsewhere in the
early chapters of the *Autobiography*. Knowing the intellectual eminence to which Mill would rise, the reader may overlook the depths
to which his father's decision had condemned him: at seventeen, he
was a junior clerk whose only distinction was that he did less scurrying to and fro than the other clerks. He was to receive no salary for
the first three years, only a gratuity of £30...By closing the prospect
of the bar as his profession, his father had not, of course, denied his
son his religion. The son still believed in the cause. What he had lost
was the opportunity to participate directly in its achievement.[9]

Mill's failure to mention his professional disappointment in the account of
his first mental crisis may have owed much to his desire not to do a dis-
service to his father's memory. But the other peculiarities in the authorized
account of the first crisis center on a player as yet off-stage in the chroni-
cle, Harriet Taylor.

While Mill had not yet met the inimitable Mrs. Taylor at the time of
the first crisis, the retrospective autobiographical account of his dejection
is a thinly disguised lesson in how he came to be opened up to new influences in his thought and feeling, and so primed for their subsequent meeting. In a sense, Mill's discussion of the importance of poetry, romanticism,
and feeling to overcoming the crisis is a discussion of how Harriet was perfect for him. The *Autobiography* account of the mental crisis is, in this way,
a crucial bit of text in the larger project of justifying an intimate associa-

---

[9] *John Stuart Mill and the Writing of Character*, (University of Georgia Press: Athens,
Georgia, 1991), p. 61.

8   *John Stuart Mill's Deliberative Landscape*

tion that threatened to blacken both his reputation and hers. Moreover, although his father was responsible for frustrating John's early political ambitions, his relationship with Harriet Taylor was at least partly to blame for his own failure to seek an alternate route into law and politics.

In his late teens and early twenties, John Stuart Mill was at the center of a remarkable group of men. His friends were both ambitious and powerful. Just as James Mill pulled strings to get a Parliamentary seat for Charles Austin,[10] several of John Stuart Mill's friends might have used their influence on his behalf. But John Stuart Mill withdrew from *anyone* in his extra-familial circle who openly expressed *any* qualms about his relations with Mrs. Taylor, and this meant withdrawing from nearly everyone who might have helped him toward law and got him a suitable post in English government.[11] Harriet and John were very anxious with these matters while he was drafting the *Autobiography* and she was telling him what to delete and what to emphasize.

The story Mill tells about his first mental crisis seems to have been shaped by anxiety about his relations with his father and Harriet. The complete omission of the second crisis from the work may have a similar explanation. The second crisis was *much* more severe than the first. It required that Mill take an extensive leave of absence from his job, and was the only time in his almost superhumanly busy life that he ever complained of overwork. Because Mill did not write about this episode at any length, it is much harder to trace its impact through his writings. But it seems to have begun at the end of his father's long illness, and come to a head in 1836, fast on the heels of James Mill's death and almost exactly ten years after the first mental crisis. Alexander Bain, John's friend, described the second crisis as "an obstinate derangement of the brain," the symptoms of which included "involuntary nervous twitchings in the face," breathing trouble, melancholy, weight loss, and extreme reluctance to carry on with work at

---

[10] See Alexander Bain, *James Mill*, (Longmans, Green, and Co.: London, 1882), p. 465.

[11] Mill still would have needed something on the order of admission to the bar to enter Parliamentary service. Seats in Parliament carried no salary and John Stuart Mill had to make a living one way or another. But lawyering was a way compatible with service in the House of Commons, and a holding bureaucratic post in East India House was not. It is unclear what a break with James Mill would have done to the fortunes of John Stuart Mill. It is pretty clear that the effects of the younger Mill's decision to do his father's bidding and insistence on maintaining an intimacy with Harriet Taylor jointly determined that John Stuart Mill would not make a name for himself first in Parliament.

Life and Work, Men and Women, Thought and Feeling 9

the Leadenhall Street office.[12] John Stuart Mill was plagued by respiratory ailments and a twitch in one eye ever afterward. He had spent much of his father's last illness torn between his duty to his father and his desire to spend time with Harriet. Shortly after his father's death, John Stuart Mill was again promoted at East India House and, once he had returned from his six month leave of absence, took over his father's position there.

There are many psychological stories that might be told about both of these events. I will tell *one* sort of story about the first mental crisis, a story that coincides with John Skorupski's sense that Mill's philosophical powers were partly to blame for its shape and outcome.[13] For, however the pressures of paternal love and ambition contributed to Mill's first episode of psychological turmoil, and however much his later relations with Harriet shaped his account of what it took to get over it, it is fairly plain that the philosophically interesting *result* of the confluence of forces in him was a major change in his thought. The change in his thought was occasioned by his discovery that something was very, very wrong with the moral psychology he had been raised on, and that had shaped his education. And how he grappled with this in writing is all by itself interesting and important, even if the account of the problem was made partly with an eye toward protecting his father and partly with an eye toward justifying the love of his life. Part of the reason to mention the circumstances surrounding the mental crises is to supply a cautionary note in before reading the account of the first in the *Autobiography*. The other part of the reason is that John Stuart Mill is often read as torn between something represented by his wife and something represented by his father.

THOUGHT AND FEELING

Now, the fact that John Stuart Mill wrote an autobiography doubtless explains something of the scholarly interest in his personal life. And the fact that the "everyone" who, Berlin tells us, "knows" the story of Mill's education will also know something about James Mill and Harriet Taylor may explain some of the emphasis that has been placed on Mill's education and singular intimate partnership. But neither the scholarly or literary merit of the *Autobiography*, nor the intellectual prominence of James Mill,

[12] *John Stuart Mill*, (Longmans, Green and Co.: London, 1882), pp. 42-44.
[13] In his study of Mill's philosophy, Skorupski remarks that Mill's "crystalline" philosophical vision was "no doubt the true cause" of the first mental crisis, then adds, in a footnote, that the crisis was "Described in the *Autobiography*, and much over-interpreted ever since" [*John Stuart Mill*, (Routledge: London, 1989), p. 13 & fn 4, p. 390].

nor even the fact that John Mill collaborated with Harriet on some of his most important work in political philosophy,[14] fully accounts for the peculiar way in which Mill's friends and foes have sometimes seen his life as relevant to his work. From his death until quite recently many of Mill's readers, after making passing reference to the intellectual ferment that characterized the exercise of public reason in mid-nineteenth century England, and to Mill's eminence, promptly reduced the formative influences on John Stuart Mill's thought to two people, James Mill and Harriet Taylor, neither of whom is much remembered for philosophical depth. Berlin mentioned the father. It is more common to find the pair discussed in connection with Mill's work. For example, Bertrand Russell wrote:

> Intellectually, [John Stuart Mill] was unfortunate in the date of his birth. His predecessors were pioneers in one direction, and his successors in another. The sub-structure of his opinions remained always that which had been laid down for him in youth by the dominating personality of his father, but the theories which he built upon this sub-structure were very largely such as it could not support. Skyscrapers, I am told, cannot be built in London because they need to be founded on rock. Mill's doctrines, like a skyscraper founded on clay, were shaky because the foundations were continually sinking. The new storeys, which he added under the inspiration of Carlyle and Mrs. Taylor, were intellectually insecure. To put the matter another way: morals and intellect were perpetually at war in his thought, morals being incarnate in Mrs. Taylor and intellect in his father. If the one was too soft, the other was too harsh. The amalgam which resulted was practically beneficent, but theoretically somewhat incoherent.[15]

And so we find the great opposition between Harriet Taylor and James Mill. The symbolic *agon* between these two is often introduced to explain the trouble in getting a consistent read on John Stuart Mill's philosophy.

[14] *On Liberty* was, for example, I think, the product of their collaboration, and *The Subjection of Women* grows out of their joint interest in women's equality. Jack Stillinger argues that Harriet's role in the writing of *On Liberty* was relatively minor [see his "Introduction" to *The Early Draft of John Stuart Mill's Autobiography*, (University of Illinois Press: Urbana, Ill., 1961)]. Mill insisted that "there was not a sentence of it that was not several times gone through by us together" (1: 257). Stillinger bases his skepticism on the manuscript evidence. But, since much of the composition took place during John and Harriet's brief marriage, it is entirely possible that they did their work in conversation. If so, it is unsurprising that her marginalia do not support Mill's insistence that the *Liberty* was a joint production.
[15] "John Stuart Mill," reprinted in *Mill: A Collection of Critical Essays*, ed. J. B. Schneewind, (University of Notre Dame Press: Notre Dame, Ind., 1969), p. 2.

Life and Work, Men and Women, Thought and Feeling 11

Now, in spite of Russell's confidence that we heirs of those unnamed pioneers in another direction have got beyond the sub-structure that rendered Mill's mature views "somewhat incoherent," the series of oppositions that Russell invokes in making his metaphor and his point suggest that some old organizing associations went along for the ride in the new direction. For by "morals" Russell clearly has in view matters of sentiment and value, figured as over-soft and under-reasoned, and, in the implicit gendering of thought and feeling that frames Russell's figure of speech, feminine (Carlyle fades from view very quickly)—in short, the stuff of doing things, not of thinking about them. By "intellect," on the other hand, Russell means the reflective, unsentimental exercise of (masculine) rational powers. But it was, I will argue, *precisely* a certain sort of separation of thought and feeling, intellect and practical direction, that was the trouble with the foundations for moral philosophy provided by the psychological theories of James Mill. The style of philosophical psychology that John Stuart Mill learned at his father's knee is as much responsible for the difficulty in sorting through his philosophical views as anything is. Crucial features of that style of thought shape Russell's own assessment of Mill.

Notice that Russell's metaphor is itself liable to sink under the slightest pressure. The problem with Mill's attempt to erect an intellectual skyscraper isn't so much that the sentimental and moral storeys were in bad shape (these were "practically beneficent," i.e., the stuff of sound action in ethics and politics). The problem was rather that the intellectual foundations provided by the elder Mill gave his son's edifice its historically unfortunate feet of clay. The too *harsh* side of John Stuart Mill's work is, in this sense, the *soft* bit, the strand of thought developed in such works as James Mill's *Analysis of the Phenomena of the Human Mind* which was unsuited to ground action or policy. The "dominant" masculine contribution to John Stuart Mill's corpus was the sinking stuff of passive impressions (clay), whereas the "inspiring" feminine contribution took definite shape as active, useful moral storeys unhappily situated over the morass of paternal matter.

Russell's implicit treatment of the conflict in Mill's thought as a symptom of failed masculinity is nothing new.[16] It has long been common to treat various features of Mill's mature philosophical views as a mark of

---

[16] For example, while John Stuart Mill held a seat in Parliament (and during his failed attempt to retain it), *Judy* ran political cartoons which portrayed him as a "timid miss" in lady's clothing. See, e.g., *Judy* (24 July 1867) and (25 March 1868). Such cartoons were in part a response to Mill's feminism, set out in some detail in his *The Subjection of Women*. The thought seems to have been that no fully realized man could advocate extensive formal equality in law for women. For instance, Herbert Cowell's review of *On Liberty* and *The Subjection of Women* suggests that some

gender trouble. Virginia Woolf's father, Leslie Stephen, put it this way:

> James Mill, whatever his faults, was a man, born to be a leader of men. He was rigid, imperative, and capable of controlling and dominating. John Stuart Mill was far weaker in that sense, and weaker because he had less virility. Mill never seems to fully appreciate the force of human passions; he fancies that the emotions which stir men to their depths can be controlled by instilling a few moral maxims or pointing out considerations of utility. He has in that respect less 'human nature' in him than most human beings.[17]

In Stephen's account, the problem is likewise an imbalance between thought and feeling, but this time the problem isn't that James Mill, the intellectual, was in error and the softer, moralizing side of John Stuart Mill's sensibility (the province of Mrs. Taylor) was sound. The problem is

of Mill's views stem from not having had experience with the need to exercise paternal authority and husbandly supervision in the "real Conditions" of married life ["Liberty, Equality, Fraternity," *Blackwood's Edinburgh Magazine*, vol. 114 (Sept. 1873), reprinted in *Liberty: Contemporary Responses to John Stuart Mill*, ed. Andrew Pyle, (Thoemmes Press: Bristol, 1994), p. 299], and Mill's much-discussed "femininity" is part of John Wilson's explanation of the doctrines in Mill's essays on liberty and women's subjection [*The Quarterly Review*, vol. 135 (1873), reprinted in *Liberty: Contemporary Responses to John Stuart Mill*, ed. Andrew Pyle, (Thoemmes Press: Bristol, 1994), pp. 321-48].

[17] *The English Utilitarians*, vol. III, (Augustus M. Kelley Publishers: New York, 1900/1968), p. 72. One might note, here, the exceeding strangeness involved in seeing a man whose job consisted in negotiating the business of India in a way that helped make possible direct imperial control by the Crown as somehow *not* exercising leadership, and somehow *failing* to make a political mark on the world commensurate with his potential. Indeed, the Parliamentary work of his friends probably had, at the end of the day, *much* less effect on the conditions of life in England than Mill's multi-volume series of "political despatches" did. It seems wildly improbable to suppose that the invisibility of India in assessing Mill's political impact and leadership potential is due to the commentators' moral squeamishness about imperialism coupled with some desire to protect Mill from being remembered principally as an architect of majestic injustice who was busily using conditions surrounding English control in India as a model of a well-ordered and well-governed society. It is hard to imagine how a current reader of his work on representative government could fail to be struck by the place of the East India Company in his thoughts, but it is equally hard to imagine that the first response to noticing the Empire in the making would be a desire to protect John Stuart Mill's memory. I think it more likely that the silence that hovers over Mill's role in India (in a lot of twentieth century commentary on his political views) is an effect of Eurocentric, imperialist ideology. Recently, readers have begun to focus again on the relations

Life and Work, Men and Women, Thought and Feeling

rather that John Stuart Mill failed to inherit his father's appreciation for the destructive power of emotion. Stephen was a generation closer to John Stuart Mill than Russell, and so closer to the lived political debates that the younger Mill helped to shape and direct. As such, Stephen's assessment of the relative virility of father and son may have had to do with the distance between the two's estimations of the likelihood that entrusting the functions of government to some favored minority would lead to a more just social order. James Mill held that *any* governing minority, no matter how well-educated or wise its members, would tend to make bad use of its power; one could not safely trust to a man's character and judgment to provide all the checks and balances needed to suit him for governmental service. John Stuart Mill had more optimism for governance by a panel of excellent legislators invested with extensive powers in recognition of their superior intellectual and moral character.[18] The younger Mill assumed that men and women well-equipped to rule, sterling individuals, might emerge from the educated middle classes in generations to come and enter governmental service. Stephen had neither John Stuart Mill's nor Russell's faith in individual attainments and finer feelings. It was obvious, Stephen thought, that beautifully educated people of good character were nevertheless vulnerable to the seductions of personal power, profit, and class interest. The Parliamentary reforms that had taken place in Mill's day and rather opened the lower House to the influence of admirable middle-class men had produced no very great improvements. Electors were still bribable. Speeches were still insincere. Power and place still seemed to hold the better part of the attention of legislators. Mill's views on how to make further, concrete improvements were on the ascendant in many ways at the time of his

---

between Mill's job and his thought. See, e.g., Carl Dawson, "John Stuart Mill and the East India Company," *Shoin Literary Studies* 22 (1988): 1-12; Lynn Zastoupil, "J. S. Mill and India," *Victorian Studies* 32 (1988): 31-54. For slightly older treatments of some of this material see Eric Stokes, *The English Utilitarians and India*, (Clarendon Press: Oxford, 1959), pp. 48-50; Abram Harris, "John Stuart Mill: Servant of the East India Company," *Canadian Journal of Economics and Political Science* 30 (1964): 185-202.

[18] For an interesting discussion of the development of John Stuart Mill's political theory and the proper place of educated persons in representative government see J. H. Burns, "J. S. Mill and Democracy, 1829-61", *Political Studies*, 5, 1957, reprinted in *Mill: A Collection of Critical Essays*, ed. J. B. Schneewind, (University of Notre Dame Press: Notre Dame, Ind., 1969), pp. 280-328. Burns emphasizes Harriet Taylor's influence in shaping the younger Mill's views at various stages.

death.[19] And while it was never the case that Mill's vision of a representative English government headed by the wisest and best of citizens was in any danger of being fully realized, Stephen's sense that experience had by now shown it manifestly unwise to expect finer government from finer men was widely shared among educated, liberal Englishmen in the last decades of the nineteenth century and first decade of the twentieth. The usual explanation for John Stuart Mill's faith in individual character in Stephen's day was that Mill was himself a very thoughtful and sober person with an abnormally large measure of integrity, a man unmoved by flattery, dutiful, unnaturally free of strong feeling, and, for the most part, open-minded.[20] The younger Mill had stuck to his theoretical guns in his one term in Parliament. The result had been his open advocacy of policies that had no hope of passing into law and his clear opposition to measures with significant legislative and popular support. He looked to have none of the skills of the practical politician, and, by the time Stephen was writing, it seemed unclear that government by many such men was apt to be any better than government as usual with one such man making speeches in the House of Commons. The usual picture of John Stuart Mill, adduced sometimes to explain his difficulties in practice, sometimes to explain the trouble with his theories, had it that his father was more intellectually uncompromising than he, his wife more romantic and emotional, and that John Stuart Mill was perpetually poised between the two.

What matters for my purposes, however, is not whether James Mill or Harriet Taylor had the more pronounced effect upon John Stuart Mill's writings, nor whether his philosophy was masculine or feminine, nor even which of two important people in his life had the more salutary effect upon his thought. I will instead concentrate upon the morals versus intellect, sentiment versus reason, soft versus harsh framework that informs both Mill's practical philosophy and Russell's sketch of why it comes to grief.

In what follows I will argue that Mill's theoretical difficulty (like Russell's description of it) belies commitment to an untenable view about the character of practical reason and moral psychology. Practical reason is

---

[19] The Irish Land Acts of 1870 and 1881, and their extension in England by the Agricultural Holdings Act bore the stamp of Mill's policy recommendations. His advocacy of women's rights was seen as crucial to the passing of three Married Women's Property Acts and the separation clauses in the Divorce Acts. His deep suspicion of the ballot as a key to deep and lasting political reform seemed confirmed by the inquiries into electoral misconduct of 1881.

[20] See, for example, Edward Jenks's 1888 essay, *Thomas Carlyle and John Stuart Mill*, (Thoemmes Press: Bristol, 1990), pp. 241-42.

Life and Work, Men and Women, Thought and Feeling 15

reason in the service of action, decision or policy. Following contemporary usage among moral philosophers I will call the untenable view at issue *instrumentalism*. Mill attempted to overcome some aspects of a broadly instrumentalist view of the human mind without casting aside its basic outlines. The resulting theoretical stance was, indeed, "somewhat incoherent," but its incoherence mirrors the incoherence in Russell's metaphor: the view depends upon affecting a separation of thought and feeling, intellect and objectives, pleasures or pains and ideas, that comes to grief variously. The rhetoric of one kind of sexual division of labor—women are in charge of emotion, morals and the maintenance of bodies; men are in charge of reason, economic competition and providing means of subsistence—may help to give the philosophical separation of thought and feeling the appearance of plausibility in the indirect, unexamined way that such things do, but this does not render the moral psychological position cogent. John Stuart Mill was both a good enough philosopher and a reflective enough person to register the strain in many and subtle ways in his work. How that strain develops, and how it makes trouble in philosophy, psychology and the living of an examined life will be my topic in this essay.

In the next chapter, I will lay out the crucial features of instrumentalism, discuss the sense in which the associationist philosophical psychology James Mill developed under Jeremy Bentham's inspiration was instrumentalist, and pave the way for a reading of John Stuart Mill.

CHAPTER 2

Instrumentalism

An Obscure Doctrine

In this chapter I will lay out and discuss a family of positions in moral philosophy that are nowadays treated under the rubric "instrumentalism," connect these views to the moral psychology that informed John Stuart Mill's education, and lay some groundwork for a central thesis in this essay: that associationism embodied a kind of moral psychological instrumentalism, and that, to the degree that John Stuart Mill retained his commitment to key features of associationist doctrine throughout his maturity, he saddled himself with a commitment to instrumentalist moral psychology. Most readers of Mill will reject these suggestions outright. Part of the burden of this chapter, then, will be to argue that, on the most charitable view of what instrumentalism comes to, it is not implausible to see it at work in associationist moral psychology.

What contemporary instrumentalism comes to, I'll argue, is in no way obvious. What contemporary instrumentalism seems always to involve, however, is some version of the great bifurcation of the mind that reared itself in Bertrand Russell's and Leslie Stephen's complaints about Mill's practical philosophy. For Russell, it was the distinction between things pertinent to thought and things pertinent to morals or practice. For Stephen, it was the divide between passion and reasoning.

I will begin this chapter by tracing some difficulties which plague the use of the term "instrumentalism," (not the least of which is that its inventor could not possible countenance its current field of application). I will go on to outline various positions in moral philosophy which are treated as expressive of instrumentalist theoretical commitments, argue that, on the

18   *John Stuart Mill's Deliberative Landscape*

face of it, they have precious little to do with one another, and then settle upon an account of instrumentalism which seems to me best to capture some features of current usage of the term. Finally, I will connect these to John Stuart Mill, Jeremy Bentham, and James Mill and begin moving into my principal areas of concern.

"INSTRUMENTALISM"

The contemporary philosophical term "instrumentalism" is an unhappy one in many ways. John Dewey, who coined the term and baptized his own his own position with it, would have had little use for the view "instrumentalism" came to designate in philosophy of science, still less for some aspects of the mishmash of vaguely interconnected "instrumentalist" positions in practical philosophy.[1] Dewey's instrumentalism was an attempt to produce a unified theory of concepts, judgments and inferences that could compass the whole of evaluative and scientific knowledge.[2] Such an attempt is, of course, predicated upon the supposition that there *is* such a thing as evaluative knowledge, and hence upon a denial of the separation of intellect and morals, inquiry and art, knowledge and value, thought and the wellsprings of action which link the various positions involved in contemporary "instrumentalist" moral philosophy.

Dewey's ambitions for a critical philosophy of instrumentalism were not realized. Instead, in one of intellectual history's little ironies, "instrumentalism" nowadays covers one thing in philosophy of science, quite another in moral philosophy. In both of its homes, it centers upon the idea that, in some sphere of activity (scientific research; rational action generally), some essential factors of practical production are objective and truth-governed (in science, data; in rational action, means-end, calculative reasoning and belief), and others have different epistemic standing (in science, theories; in rational action, desires or ends). While at this abstract level of description it might seem that the two sorts of views have something

---

[1] I am grateful to Michael Williams for urging me to investigate Dewey's instrumentalism.

[2] See, for example, *John Dewey, The Middle Works. 1899-1924*, ed. Jo Ann Boydston (Southern Illinois University Press: Carbondale, Ill., 1976-83), vol. 10, p. 366. Part of the difficulty Dewey faced in making his project clear to his contemporaries was just the seductiveness of a vision of the mind as having distinct intellectual and desiderative components. The view undergirded an idea that science involved the "pure" exercise of rational powers, and made it seem to Dewey's readers that, by distancing himself from the vision of the purity of science and its associated theory of truth, Dewey was impugning the intellect by sullying it with a crass desiderative taint.

Instrumentalism 19

important in common, they are very, very different. Among other things, instrumentalist moral philosophers are inclined to look upon the whole product and process of scientific research as the fruit of plain reason directed at truth. Instrumentalist philosophers of science are unlikely to suppose that the peculiar epistemic standing of theoretical statements marks them as the deliverance of subjective desires or expressions of private ends. But both the divergence of instrumentalism in philosophy of science from instrumentalism in moral philosophy, and the tendency in each domain to see instrumentalism as involving the thought that there are two important ingredients to the phenomena under consideration, one of which is truth-governed, the other of which is not, attest to the tremendous resilience of a division of psychological labor into a sphere of past experience and plain reasoning and a sphere more concerned with value and future-directed action, in Russell's parlance, "intellect" and "morals."

In philosophy of science, "instrumentalism" came to be associated with the view that scientific theories are instruments for rendering observation statements systematic and for deriving some sets of observation statements (predictions) from others (data). Nowadays, instrumentalist views of science treat theoretical entities as useful fictions, and have it that observation statements are truth-valued, whereas theoretical statements, while useful for doing science (and in this sense, "practically beneficent"), are neither true nor false.[3]

Hereafter, by "instrumentalism" I will mean instrumentalism in practical philosophy. Instrumentalism on *this* side—instrumentalism about ethics, moral psychology and practical reason—is more slippery. In the first departure from Dewey, instrumentalism came to center on the thought that sentences expressing some judgments of value could be reformulated as statements expressing relationships between means and ends; the means-ends statements, in turn, could be stripped of evaluative or prescriptive terminology, and so rendered susceptible of empirical test.[4] For example, the

---

[3] One difference between Dewey's instrumentalism and the instrumentalism developed by the positivist philosophers of science was that the positivist view concentrated on the status of scientific theories *over and against* observation statements, focusing on the claim that theoretical statements were used in making inferences about observation statements. The epistemic status of observation statements was secure in a way that the epistemic status of theoretical statements was not. For Dewey, "instrumental" did not mark a contrast of epistemic status and inferential role among kinds of statements. Quite the contrary, anything known was known insofar as it contributed to successful inference.

[4] For an example of this reworking of Dewey's position about practical philosophy and empirical judgment see Carl Hempel, *Aspects of Scientific Explanation*, (The Free

thought goes, sentences like "It would be good for us to eat at home tonight" or "We ought to eat at home tonight" could be reformulated as conditionals expressing "relative" or "instrumental" practical judgments, such as "If we are to save money, then it would be good to eat in," or "If we are to continue this dispute over supper, and we prefer not to fight in crowded places, then we ought to eat in." The conditionals could then be recast as statements about means and ends: "Means M (eating in) definitely or probably will lead to the realization of end E (saving money; securing food and privacy)." The means-end statements were empirically testable, unlike (it was thought) the initial prescriptive or evaluative judgments.

This method of moving from evaluative statements to causal generalizations of some sort turned on a smallish thought open to the usual concerns about the status of reformulations. The proffered means weren't the only means to the ends in question—one could save still more money by going without supper entirely; one could eat and argue on a drive, or on a lonely park bench, or by the sea. There was no claim that the means were the "best" or "most efficient" means to the ends in question. Any such claim about the special merit of some means involves a *further* evaluative judgment—"best" is a value term, and, in this context, "most efficient" likewise suggests that the means in question are especially valuable. It is *much* harder to reformulate statements about which means are "better" or "more efficient" as empirically testable causal generalizations than it is to recast other evaluative statements as statements about means and ends. One way of trying to handle a claim that some means is the best means to an end might involve complicated probabilistic inferences about which course of action is *most likely* to lead to the sought-for result. The first problem in rendering *this* thought empirically testable is that there may be indefinitely many things that one *could* do to get some result. Elizabeth Anscombe made the point by considering a syllogism on the order of "Do whatever is conducive to avoiding a car crash/ Such-and-such is conducive to avoiding a car crash/ Ergo: do such-and-such" rehearsed while driving a car. She commented:

> someone professing to accept the premises will be inconsistent if, when nothing intervenes to prevent him, he fails to act on the particular order with which the argument ends. But this syllogism suffers from the disadvantage that the first, universal, premise is an insane one, which no one could accept for a minute if he thought out what it meant. For there are usually a hundred different and incompatible things conducive to not having a car crash; such as, perhaps, driving into the private gateway immediately on your left and aban-

Press: New York, 1965), pp. 84-90.

Instrumentalism 21

> doning your car there, and driving into the private gateway immedi-
> ately on your right and abandoning the car there.[5]

Outside the artifices of mathematical models of choice, where the set of available actions and ends can be duly constrained by postulates of one sort or another—and it is unclear that such models yield empirically testable casual generalizations in the first place—one obvious way to try to render the choice set less unwieldy is by restricting it to the means that an agent considers taking to her end. One problem with doing so is that if I never consider more than one means to any end (I am, say, lazy, unimaginative or dim-witted), then *whatever* I decide to do in any case where I actually decide to do something that has some hope of success, however faint, will automatically count as the "best" or "most efficient" means to my end. Which in turn suggests that one way of "optimizing" my choices will be by blinding myself to the lion's share of my options. That *can't* be what the friends of efficiency have in mind. But it isn't clear how to get an account of anything they *might* have in mind by relying upon the small thought about means and ends, either.

And what of the end? The end was treated as a result which the agent aimed to bring about by taking the relevant means. Not all ends have this character. The most obvious exceptions are activities or courses of action which are themselves ends. Consider: "It would be good to take a stroll" or "I ought to take a stroll." An attempt to "reformulate" these sentences as conditionals expressing instrumental practical judgments will be at best strained. Suppose, as is often the case, that there is *no* further end served by taking a casual stroll, that one simply wants to go for a walk, that walking itself is pleasant or invigorating, where neither the pleasure nor the sense of vigor in walking is best grasped as a further *result* to be brought about *by* walking. Walking involves putting one foot in front of another, and one could try: "If I want to walk, then I must put one foot in front of the other," recasting this as "Means M (putting one foot in front of the other) proba-bly or definitely will lead to the realization of end E (taking a walk)." Notice, however, that since the conditions under which putting one foot in front of the other "lead to" walking are ordinarily conditions under which putting one foot in front of the other just *is* walking, the reformulation does not look to give us a standard means-end statement at all. Evaluative or prescriptive sentences involving ends wanted for their own sakes resist means-ends reformulation. But then, as I noted, the thought that some sen-tences containing prescriptive or evaluative terms could be recast as state-

---

[5] Anscombe, *Intention*, (Cornell University Press: Ithaca, NY, 1963), §33. She draws the example from some remarks by R. M. Hare.

ments about means and ends was a small thought. It did not include the attempt to argue that the reformulation strategy could be applied to every sentence expressing a prescriptive or evaluative judgment, nor even that every sentence containing evaluative or prescriptive terms was best interpreted as expressing a practical judgment involving a determinate end.

INSTRUMENTALISM IN CONTEMPORARY MORAL PHILOSOPHY

The small thought about means and ends had this much going for it: it was reasonably precise and carried remnants of Dewey's pragmatism with it. Things have got much more muddled in recent use of "instrumentalism" in moral philosophy. The term has come to cover something more like a philosophical mood than a definite position, and that mood is expansive. That contemporary moral philosophical instrumentalism is indefinite reveals itself in the recent tendency to categorize philosophers who lived and died centuries before Dewey, with whom Dewey had little in common, and whose own views likewise diverge—like Hobbes and Hume—as instrumentalists. That contemporary instrumentalism in practical philosophy is expansive is shown by the sheer breadth of topics treated under its rubric:

1. instrumentalism can be a view about practical reasoning—the view that practical reasoning consists solely in calculating which means best will serve which ends; that there is no deliberation of ends, but only of means; or
2. instrumentalism can be a view about the metaphysics of value—usually the view that human nature, culture and desire are the only possible sources of value on a properly scientific world view; or
3. instrumentalism can be a view about reasons for acting—let 'A' indicate action of type A, then instrumentalism centers on the claim that one has a reason for A-ing only if A-ing is a means to or part of attaining one or more of one's determinate further ends; or
4. instrumentalism can involve any of several positions in moral psychology.

The various topics and views in practical philosophy that are nowadays designated as "instrumentalist" have some connection to each other. For instance, one could hold *all* of the positions I've outlined without falling into an obvious inconsistency. Nevertheless, it is equally possible to pick and choose among the four without taking on the whole bundle. I might be a metaphysical realist about value who held that some ends are ration-

Instrumentalism 23

ally desirable in themselves but that there is no deliberation of ends (as Aquinas is). I might hold that human nature and human culture are the sources of value in the world and that there *is* deliberation of ends (as does Bernard Williams). I might hold that there is some clear distinction to be drawn between the operation of sentiment and the operation of plain reason and be a realist about value (one who held, e.g., that one or more sentimental powers tracked material truths about values and that some intellectual power was, strictly, devoted to grasping abstract relations among things), allow that there *is* such a thing as deliberation of ends, but deny that one has reason to do anything without some determinate end in view (Bishop Butler's view is rather like this). Etc.

Part of the difficulty, then, in defending instrumentalism in moral philosophy (as hardly anyone does) or inveighing against it (as has become breathtakingly common of late) is just that the cluster of views organized under its banner need bear no necessary relations one to another. Worse yet, there is scarcely any agreement about which topic (or, for that matter, which position on the relevant topic) is crucial to contemporary instrumentalism. Elijah Millgram, for instance, takes Robert Audi's views on practical reason as a paradigmatic instance of instrumentalism because Audi holds that practical reasoning is concerned with matching means to ends.[6] In the work to which Millgram refers, Audi thrice denies instrumentalism on the grounds that some ends are rationally desirable in themselves.[7]

In the face of this sort of thing, and in deference to Dewey, it might be thought better to simply dispense with the term "instrumentalism" altogether. I won't. But I will reserve the use of "instrumentalism" for positions in moral psychology that depend upon the separation of affect and intellect and the view that the psychological antecedents of human action are such that there can be no rational grounding for primary ends. As I will understand it, instrumentalism has it that ends are supplied by what one wants and that practical reason is exercised in order to make the world be as one wants it to be or stay as one wants it to stay. Affect supplies ends. Intellect supplies ways of attaining ends. End of story. Some ways of elaborating upon this story produce elegant, formal models of reason in action. The formal models generally concentrate on relations between ends represented as ordered preferences.[8]

---

[6] Millgram, *Practical Induction*, (Harvard University Press: Cambridge, Mass., 1997), p. 4.

[7] Audi, *Practical Reasoning*, (Routledge: London, 1989), pp. 179, 183, 191.

[8] In effect, the models treat ordered groups of ends as single, complex primary ends,

24   *John Stuart Mill's Deliberative Landscape*

Here's why I will focus on the psychological framework and its attendant picture of the limited role of reason in action. First off, when push comes to shove, defenders and detractors of instrumentalism alike are apt to point to a view in moral psychology as the crucial element of instrumentalism. For instance, David Gauthier begins laying out his avowedly instrumentalist conception of practical reason with what appears to be a thesis about the metaphysics of value, and quickly locates the allure of instrumentalism in its moral psychological "base":

> 'There is nothing good or bad, but thinking makes it so.' But if things considered in themselves are neither good not bad, if there is no realm of value existing independently of animate beings and their activities, then thought is not the activity that summons value into being. Hume reminds us, 'Reason is, and ought only to be the slave of the passions', and while Hume's dictum has been widely disputed, we shall defend it. Desire, not thought, and volition, not cognition, are the springs of good and evil.[9]

In explaining the appeal of instrumentalism, Millgram, a staunch anti-instrumentalist, writes:

> How could anything be a reason for action if it could not motivate you to actually *do* something? And what could motivate you to do something except one of your desires? [Instrumentalism] seems refreshingly honest: People who try to convince you to do things you don't want to do are, too often, just trying to bully you into doing something you don't really have any reason to do at all. Instrumentalism seems to give you a very convenient way to distinguish this kind of browbeating from real reasons to act: real reasons bottom out in what you want anyway. And instrumentalism seems to be metaphysically respectable, where the arbiter of respectability in the relevant circles is a broadly-shared image of science. Desires are psychological states, and there is no problem in making room for psychological states among the particles, organisms, causal regularities, and other items we encounter in science textbooks;[10]

Partly because the psychological aspect of the bundle of instrumentalist

---

and investigate such matters as strategies by which an agent can expect to attain them, the basis for bargaining or negotiation they provide, the trade-offs commensurate with the ranking of component secondary ends, and how that ranking is sensitive to the probability of attaining the complex primary end or its constituent secondary ends.

[9] *Morals By Agreement*, (Clarendon Press: Oxford, 1986), p. 21.

[10] *Practical Induction*, (Harvard University Press: Cambridge, Mass., 1997), pp. 4-5.

Instrumentalism 25

views in moral philosophy has special place in the assessment of the view, I will take it that instrumentalism is primarily a position in philosophical psychology generally, moral psychology more specifically, about the limited role of human reason in shaping desire, character, and, hence, the ends of action. In short, I will call "instrumentalism" what Warren Quinn calls the "neo-Humean conception of rationality." Quinn writes:

> By *neo-Humean* conception of rationality I mean one that makes the goal of practical reason...satisfaction of an agent's desires and preferences, suitably corrected for the effects of misinformation, wishful thinking, and the like. There are various versions of neo-Humean theory...Their common essence lies in an appeal (1) to a notion of *basic* desires or preferences, which are not subject to intrinsic criticism as irrational and are subject to extrinsic criticism only by ways in which their joint satisfaction may not be possible, and (2) to a notion of *derived* desires or preferences, which are criticizable only instrumentally.[11]

Basic desires line up with primary ends. Derived desires, with secondary ends (wanted as means to or parts of attaining primary ends). Derived desires are instrumentally criticizable—i.e., one's reason for satisfying them vanishes if one learns that attaining the secondary ends that are their objects is neither a means to nor a part of attaining one's primary ends and so satisfying basic desires. Primary ends, the objects of basic desires, are not rationally criticizable. That is, that there are no reasons for primary ends. Quinn's characterization nicely captures the intimacy of the moral psychology and the view about reasons for acting.

That various views about the mind are tightly linked with a particular picture of practical reason in contemporary work is one reason to focus on instrumentalism as a position in moral psychology. Equally importantly however, is this. One thing that those diverse "instrumentalist" figures in the history of English language moral philosophy *share* is a tradition of psychological theorizing. Hobbes and Hume have very different views about ethics and political theory.[12] Hobbes held, for example, that there

---

[11] "Rationality and the Human Good," in *Morality and Action*, (Cambridge University Press: Cambridge, 1993), pp. 210-11. I have omitted reference to maximal preference satisfaction in this quote. Quinn explicitly connects neo-Humeanism to *maximizing* accounts of rationality. There seems no very clear reason to do so. It is not as though accounts of rationality couched in terms of "satisficing" or "regret-minimization" rather than the maximization of preference satisfaction embody a fundamentally *different* picture of means, ends, and the psychological roots of reasons for acting.

[12] Contemporary Hume scholars have argued that Hume is not, in fact, an instru-

26   *John Stuart Mill's Deliberative Landscape*

are no motives or sentiments that differ in their kind or their objects from self-love. In insisting that virtue could not be reduced to a species of self-love, Hume held that moral sentiments differed in their objects and kind from Hobbist egoistic affective states. (This feature of Hume's position was to be echoed by John Stuart Mill in his defense of utilitarianism.) But, however divergent their positions in moral philosophy, Hobbes and Hume alike belong to a long line of philosophical psychologists who were engaged with some of the same basic theses about the character of the human mind.[13]

In the Preface to the 1869 edition of his father's *Analysis of the Phenomena of the Human Mind*, John Stuart Mill wrote:

> The analytic study of the facts of the human mind...was first carried to considerable height by Hobbes and Locke, who are the real founders of the view of the Mind which regards the greater part of its intellectual structure as having been built up by Experience...Dr. Hartley's treatise (*Observations on Man*) goes over the whole field of mental phenomena, both intellectual and emotional, and points out the way in which, as he thinks, sensations, ideas of sensation, and association, generate and account for the principal complications of our mental nature...[But Hartley] encumbered his theory of Association with a premature hypothesis respecting the physical mechanism of sensation and thought [and his] book is made up of hints rather than of proofs...It was another great disadvantage to Hartley's theory, that its publication so nearly coincided with the commencement of the reaction against the Experience psychology, provoked by the hardy skepticism of Hume (31: 97-98).

To James Mill, John Stuart adds, "the honour belongs of being the reviver and second founder of the Associationist psychology" (31: 99). What unites Hobbes, Locke, Hume and the Mills with the less well-remembered Dr. Hartley, Erasmus Darwin, and Joseph Priestley is a tradition of psychological work.[14]

In this sense, focusing upon the moral psychological dimension of instrumentalism not only captures something of the special emphasis on psychology in contemporary debates, but explains how the use of the term seems naturally to extend backwards along a line of thinkers who in other

---

mentalist. Still, so-called "Humean" or "neo-Humean" accounts of motivation are paradigmatic exercises in instrumentalist moral psychology.

[13] For a lucid, broad, and fascinating discussion of the relevant line of work in psychology, see Fred Wilson, *Psychological Analysis and the Philosophy of John Stuart Mill*, (University of Toronto Press: Toronto, 1990), pp. 20-83.

[14] For references to Darwin and Priestley see Mill (31: 98).

Instrumentalism 27

ways have very little in common. The contemporary instrumentalist mood, that is, is most naturally expressed in a style of philosophical psychology that sets severe limitations on the role of reason in action, buttressed by a conviction that views about ethics, political theory and practical reason can be independently grounded in philosophical psychology.

The idea that philosophical psychology holds the key to sound views about ethics and practical reason may have become so common that the reader will wonder where else one *could* go to get a grip on these topics. It is well beyond the scope of this essay to say where. What I will say is this: there is a distinction between the modest claim that in doing moral philosophy we are engaged with topics that involve thought, judgment, character traits, emotions, etc. (which is true) and the much more ambitious claim that empirical, scientific or philosophical study of mental phenomena is sufficient for answering questions about practical reason and ethics. My suspicion is that the ambitious claim is false, and that any appearance of truth it might have stems from the difficulty of coming up with a framework for psychological speculation that does not already embody crucial features of a doctrine about practical reason (which may or may not have ethical implications). Part of the purpose of this essay will be to argue that the associationist moral psychology of James and John Stuart Mill, for instance, was at the same time an instrumentalist account of practical reason.

CONNECTING CONTEMPORARY WORK TO EARLIER WORK

I am interested in one aspect of the large, sometimes interconnected, bundle of instrumentalist views in moral philosophy. That aspect involves a tendency to divide the mind into a cognitive part or faculty or power and an affective part or faculty or power and to argue that the character of the division is such as to preclude the possibility of rational support for ultimate ends. The mode of division that will occupy me in what follows has its historical roots in the tradition of empiricist moral psychology stretching back at least to Hobbes, and continuing (at least) through the development of experimental introspective psychology in the work of John Stuart Mill and Alexander Bain, given increasingly physiological emphasis in the work of Wilhelm Wundt.

By the late eighteenth-century in this tradition, the cognitive power is understood as what is exercised in perceptual judgment, in causal judgment, in judgment about the logical relations among ideas, and in analyzing or associating ideas and impressions. The affective part of mental life is understood as involving the experience of complex or simple sensations, pleasures and pains, and the associations of pleasure or pain with ideas or impressions. Volition involves both. Volition centers on desire for an end, E. Desire for E is a complex psychological state and can be analyzed into its components. In the work of the elder Mill, chief components are the *idea* of E and an associated feeling of *pleasure* (or, perhaps, relief from some occurrent pain or avoidance of some pain in prospect). The association is rooted in a causal inference based upon past experience. The causal inference concerns past action aimed at attaining ends of the relevant type (attaining such ends was pleasant or attaining such ends relieved pain). There is also a suggestion that it is based sometimes upon experience of how things went, pleasure- and pain-wise, when one *failed* to take steps to attain the relevant sorts of ends. (Ignore, here, the difficulty of determining the effects of *not* doing something; it *is* a problem, but not one which will concern me.) Given the desire for E, intellect then supplies any further casual reasoning required to determine how to attain E, or associated memory reminds one how E has been reliably attained (by oneself or by others). E itself may involve assisting others, righting wrongs, paying debts, or what have you. While, on this view, one's own happiness (understood as pleasure and the exemption from pain) is taken to be the ultimate end of one's actions, there need be no suggestion that it is always the *proximate* or *direct* primary end of each action. Nor is there any suggestion that having a desire needs to be experienced *as* seeking a pleasure or seeking to avoid or relieve a pain. Rather, analysis of the complex volitional state reveals its affective and cognitive components, and these involve associations of pleasure or pain-avoidance/pain-relief with the idea of attaining ends of the relevant sort.

In this way, the psychological anatomy of the volitional state lines up with a picture about the ultimate end of human affairs (happiness understood as the greatest balance of pleasure over pain) and an instrumental view of practical justification. The proximate and direct end of action is the attainable objective at issue (E). E may itself be pleasure or relief from pain in prospect (or avoidance of a pain that one will suffer if one takes no steps to alter one's course)—e.g., the cake looks delicious so I have some; my arm hurts so I rub it. But E might not be—e.g., you are hungry so I give you some delicious food to eat; your arm hurts so I rub it. Even if E does not *directly* involve the production of a state of pleasure or the relief or exemption from pain *in the agent*, such motivational force as the idea of attaining E has is rooted in and explained by association of the agent's pleasure or pain-exemption with attaining ends of this sort (I was made to feel bad if

Instrumentalism 29

I let people go hungry, say, or *I* was rewarded for having relieved others' pain—in James Mill's psychological analyses, *these* associated feelings-in-prospect remain *components* of my volitional state even if I do not experience them as such). Action directed at attaining an end of the relevant sort becomes a means to or part of attaining E. Attaining E is a means to or part of attaining my own happiness. And the instrumental pattern of justification for action becomes isomorphic with the component-by-component analysis of the volitional state. The ultimate end in rational action over the course of a life is the greatest balance of pleasure over pain. The proximate, primary ends (objectives) sought in human action are sought either because they promise felt pleasure directly (or the avoidance or relief from felt pain), or else because the agent has come to associate pleasure, pain-relief, or pain-avoidance with attaining them, even though the objective itself isn't the production of a feeling for the agent. There is no reason to seek happiness. We are, by nature, hedonic calculators, and practically rational action is action directed by sound hedonic calculation.

There are at least two sorts of things that might go wrong with a life lived in accordance with calculative practical reason on this view. First, one's system of associations might have been distorted by bad education or bad experience. For instance, if I am praised or petted in my childhood or youth for conduct that is more likely to bring pain than pleasure to me and most of those around me in the long run, I will wind up expecting pleasure—at least the pleasure of affection or praise—from acts which more usually bring pain and disapprobation. Sound sentimental education is required to get the associative system up and running in good order. Secondly, I may face circumstances so hostile that virtually none of my options promises much in the way of positive pleasure, and the best I can hope for, even in light of a fabulously good sentimental education, is minimizing considerable suffering. Still, barring educational or circumstantial misfortune, a life conducted on the basis of sound causal reasoning about means and ends, based in sound induction (a practically rational life) ought to be a pleasant, enjoyable life on this view. The moral psychological system is oriented toward enjoyment overall, and rational action always has in it an element of pleasure or freedom from pain in prospect, even if neither pleasure nor pain-avoidance is the direct end of each action.

Now, admittedly, one finds precious little speculation on associations of ideas, impressions, pleasures and pains in contemporary moral philosophy. The elaborate systems generated by analyses of the contents of the mind in classical British psychology are not our systems. The hedonism of classical economic theory, likewise, has been replaced by a picture of utility as a measure of preference-satisfaction, where "preferences" are no longer taken to be particular sorts of mental states with a distinctively warm emotional (or juicy motivational) tone. There is not even a suggestion that some *component* of a preference will invariably have a pleasant affective tone. That I am successfully performing actions which conduce to my maximal preference-satisfaction, for example, carries no implication that I am enjoying myself, still less that I am putting myself in the way of experiencing distinctive feelings of pleasure or ducking some sort of pain. In short, instrumentalist moral psychology has cooled down considerably of late. Rather than adverting to complex mental states composed of (although not necessarily experienced as involving) pleasures or pains, ideas, and impressions, contemporary instrumentalists point to beliefs and preferences, or beliefs and desires, or beliefs and pro-attitudes, or preferences and subjective probabilities in order to explain the mental antecedents of rational action. Analysis of the practical capacities of this cooler head is generally handled by treating beliefs, desires, or what have you, as functional or dispositional states of the subject. Each sort of state makes a distinctive contribution to action. For the instrumentalist, however, the distinctive contributions of belief-ish and desiderative mental states to action or decision are divvied up along lines that would do a classical empiricist psychologist proud. Which is why a theorist like Gauthier can quote Hume's dictum with approval and go on to develop a neo-Hobbist moral theory that draws heavily upon contemporary formal work in decision and choice, and why Quinn can describe as *neo-Humean* an account of the psychological antecedents of rational action couched in terms of the satisfaction of corrected preferences/desires (i.e., preferences/desires *not* formed in light of false beliefs—"misinformation"—or tainted beliefs—"wishful thinking and the like"). The terms have changed. The specific catalogue of kinds of mental states has changed. The division of the mind into a cognitive side and an affective or a desiderative side is somehow still in place, as is the kind of conclusion drawn about the impotence of reason in setting ends.

In a form crude to the point of something like idiocy, instrumentalism might have it that our objectives or goals or ends spring from a pool of affective states that are themselves completely impervious to the influence of judgment, thought, and reasoning, that the role of reason in human life is *not* to tell us what to seek or avoid—not even by means of the causal reasoning embedded in high-end associationist analyses of desire—but rather to direct us how best to attain the objectives given by our flatly a-rational desires, feelings, urges, aversions, tastes, or habits. Ultimately, reason cannot tell us what to want. At best and at the end of the day, all that reason

Instrumentalism 31

can do is advise us how to get or do the things we find ourselves stuck with wanting. Taken to an extreme, the view would depend upon a strict separation of thought and desire, intellect and feeling, belief and desire. Look for the source of a man's goals and you will find his desires. Ask after why he desires what he desires and, unless he desires it as a means to or part of satisfying some further desire, you will find raw, unreasoned motivational power, the sort of thing Leslie Stephen may have had in mind in adverting to the "force of human passions" and the "emotions which stir men to their depths"—elemental urges, drives, or some such which, when sufficiently stirred, produce beasts within men that cannot be directed or controlled by instilling a few reasoned maxims in the properly virile human agent. Stephen suggested that any man who has enough of the raw material of "human" nature in him can affirm the impotence of reason in controlling desire by simple introspection.

As ought to have been clear from Stephen's complaint, John Stuart Mill did *not* hold this sort of view of the human mind. Contrary to Stephen's suggestion, however, James Mill didn't hold such a view either. It is difficult to imagine that a serious philosophical psychologist *could* maintain such a position consistently. The problems with the view are various. One of them is just this: reasoning, whether practical or otherwise, is reasoning *about* some topic. If that topic is how to *satisfy* a want, even a want that has erupted onto the scene of the mental theater from a veritable witches' brew of elemental drives, then that want must present itself as directed at some object. At the very least, there must be some represented thing or state of affairs the acquisition or bringing-about of which would constitute satisfying the want. *Ex hypothesi* thinking out how to get what you want here counts as practical reasoning. *Ex hypothesi* the mental states in question, desires, can inform practical reasoning. And this in turn requires that the desires one seeks to satisfy, and thinks about how to satisfy, be contentful. Once it is admitted that these affective states are (as sources of ends, anyway)[15] contentful, it is hard to see how to maintain that they are likewise *entirely* impervious to the influence of one's cognitive powers. The suggestion is that no mere apprehension of fact, no mere thought or idea or mental image, is enough to nonaccidentally alter one's primary ends. Volition and cognition, desire and thought, affect and intel-

---

[15] Some variants of Freudian theory hold that elemental drives do not, in and of themselves, have objects, that trajectories of desire do not begin from points that are, in the relevant sense, contentful. Once they have fixed upon objects, once ends are at stake, however, desires are contentful. See, e.g., Leo Bersani, *The Freudian Body*, (Columbia University Press: New York, 1986).

lect belong to completely separate departments of mental life. This seems untrue in even cases where we have a highly impressionable agent who is deeply susceptible to strong feeling. Such a view could not really even account for what Quinn gestured toward in requiring that basic desires be "corrected" for the effects of misinformation and faulty cognitive processes. The process of rational correction even of this simple sort—e.g., I vividly, acutely crave to drink the contents of that glass, you point out that the glass contains deadly poison, I am not suicidal and so shift my attention elsewhere—requires that my desires shift systematically in response to what I learn about the world around me.[16] It also requires that the contents of my desires be brought into inferential relations one with another (that I don't want to die and that drinking the stuff in that glass will likely kill me is supposed to have some influence on my initial motive to drink it). Indeed, emotionally volatile persons are as likely to *overcorrect* in the face of new information as they are to persist in their old pursuits—confronted with the fact about what's in the glass, the calm person looks for something else to drink; the nervous person may instead lose his thirst entirely at the thought that he has had a brush with mortality. Overcorrecting in the face *of* new information is akin to overreacting *to* that information. The close tie between the two is enough to raise doubts about one very crude form of instrumentalism.

---

[16] Millgram makes the centrality of the need to learn from experience and the defeasibility of practical considerations centerpieces in his argument against instrumentalism. See *Practical Induction*, (Harvard University Press: Cambridge, Mass., 1997). His work on desire is predicated upon an argument that instrumentalism is indeed committed to a version of the position that I have described as crude to the point of idiocy. The argument is not directly relevant to the versions of instrumentalist moral psychology that I will be working through by way of reading John Stuart Mill. Millgram's instrumentalist holds that what Quinn calls "basic" desires are mental states that "one just *has*" (p. 16). Millian desires, even Millian "basic" desires, are complex states with an associative history involving inductive inference. Certain pleasures and pains are states that one just *has*, but these are not by themselves volitional. Oddly, Millgram's own view bears some striking resemblance to the sophisticated moral psychology one finds in the work of both John Stuart and James Mill. Pleasure is, for Millgram, the rock-bottom starting point for judgments about desirability, and operates as a control on attempts to argue you into wanting things that are bad for you (e.g., if someone is trying to argue you into persisting in a course that is not only making you miserable, but is unlikely ever to get any better and promises no larger good to you that might, say, be somehow enjoyable in the future, then we have an instance of bullying rather than reasoning taking place). John Stuart Mill would not have disagreed.

Instrumentalism

BENTHAMITE INSTRUMENTALISM

There is another direction that crude instrumentalism in moral psychology might take. And that direction is the one John Stuart Mill came to see in the work of his father's mentor, Jeremy Bentham. In an early essay, John Stuart Mill described Bentham's position this way:

> The first principles of Mr. Bentham's philosophy are these;—that happiness, meaning by that term pleasure and the exemption from pain, is the only thing desirable in itself; that all other things are desirable solely as a means to that end: that the production, therefore, of the greatest possible happiness, is the only fit purpose of all human thought and action, and consequently of all morality and government; and moreover, that pleasure and pain are the sole agencies by which the conduct of mankind is in fact governed, whatever circumstances the individual may be placed in, and whether he is aware of it or not (10: 5).

Mill came to conclude that there are two crucial features of this position that make it an inadequate basis for moral theory, however suited it was to guide legislation. The first was that it focused upon isolated actions of various kinds and their consequences. The second was that, in virtue of this focus on *consequences* of particular actions of specific kinds, it saw the motivational springs of action in terms of a simple calculus of pleasure and exemption from pain *in prospect*. *This* view really was open to the charge that utilitarianism implied Hobbist egoism about human motivation (a charge that Mill was at pains to rebut in *Utilitarianism*). For although the *object* of my act might be to relieve your suffering at some cost to myself, the *point* of doing so, the proximate and direct primary end of my action, is that it promises me pleasure in prospect, or else that neglecting to do so will result in some inner dissatisfaction on my part. Hedonic self-interest is the motivational force underlying human action. Bentham's critics held that, far from providing an adequate account of rational morality, the position entailed that there was no such thing as moral action.[17]

Bentham's emphasis on actions of various kinds was an emphasis on

---

[17] See, e.g., Thomas Babington Macaulay's 1829 article on James Mill's views, "Mill's Essay on Government: Utilitarian Logic and Politics," in eds. J. Lively and J. Rees, *Utilitarian Logic and Politics*, (Oxford University Press: London, 1978). Part of John Stuart Mill's task in defending utilitarianism from such critics was to make room for moral motivation in a moral psychology that involved associations between pleasures, pains, and ideas at its core. As I mentioned earlier, some of the resources for such a view could be found in Hume.

34 *John Stuart Mill's Deliberative Landscape*

determinate ends (objects) of various kinds.[18] Actions were, all alike, treated as means to pleasure or means to the relief or avoidance of pain. Crude instrumentalism focuses upon determinate primary ends—objectives—and sees these as arising (willy-nilly, in the most extreme variant of the view) from a pool of urges, drives, feelings, or what have you, which have somehow attached themselves to actions in prospect. Bentham adverts to the natural history of a person's associative system in order to explain how pleasure attaches to actions in prospect, but Benthamite utilitarianism in political and legal theory did not seek to change the springs of action "from the inside," as it were, but rather to change the external circumstances agents faced, so that their own calculations of pleasure and pain in prospect would shift direction away from actions deemed harmful to general happiness. The thought behind the legislative recommendations is simple: if everyone's end is pleasure and the avoidance of pain, action-by-action, and if you attach penalties (prospective pain) to actions of some kind which might otherwise promise pleasure to some agents, then the rational expectations of pleasure and pain attaching to actions of the kinds in question will change accordingly and the result will be to deter agents inclined to destructive or disorderly or otherwise harmful actions. You don't thereby alter agents' basic desires. What you do is make it less likely that some actions will continue to appear to be means to satisfying basic desires. Basic desires, primary ends, remain fixed by pleasure in prospect and the avoidance of pain. But, under appropriately directed educational and legislative measures, the world shifts so that some actions no longer serve as good means to those ends.

The position belies an underlying commitment to the view that reason in action is *strictly* calculative. Moreover, that the calculation is strictly governed by pleasure and pain in prospect. It is not as though, for example, you could alter an adult's motivational system with a good argument. The best you can do is alter the likelihood that actions of some sort will bring pleasure. *That* people seek pleasure is given by human nature. *Where* they seek it is given by facts about their associative systems. Education might shape the system early on, inclining people to take pleasure in actions conducive to the general welfare, but once you are confronted with adults, the die is cast. If reason is to keep *adults* on the straight and narrow, it will have to be through their causal, calculative judgments about which

---

[18] One very important way of individuating actions is in terms of their ends or goals—for example, the differences between things one does in order to make stew and things one does in order to make soup owes much to the difference between soup and stew.

Instrumentalism 35

acts will be pleasant to do or which states of affairs will be pleasant or less painful if brought about, and, barring irrational expectations, *that* means that legislators will have to arrange it so that harmful actions open the door to painful penalties.

Highlighting the crudely instrumentalist character of the view, Isaiah Berlin puts the point starkly (but, perhaps, unfairly):

> James Mill and Bentham had wanted literally nothing but pleasure obtained by whatever means were the most effective. If someone had offered them a medicine which could scientifically be shown to put those who took it into a state of permanent contentment, their premisses would have bound them to accept this as the panacea for all that they thought evil. Provided that the largest possible number of men receive lasting happiness, or even freedom from pain, it should not matter how this is achieved. Bentham and Mill believed in education and legislation as the roads to happiness. But, if a shorter way had been discovered, in the form of pills to swallow, techniques of subliminal suggestion, or other means of conditioning human beings in which our century has made such strides, then, being men of fanatical consistency, they might well have accepted this as a better, because more effective and perhaps less costly, alternative than the means that they had advocated.[19]

Notice, again, the tight connection between the moral psychological view about pleasure and the view of practical reason as narrowly calculative. Notice too that one of the main objections to this view is that it fails to supply a rational grounding for proximate or ultimate ends. Every action aims (if only indirectly) at pleasure or relief from pain. Every action is thus a *means* to these. Ask why we ought to set such store by pleasure and the only answer is that we are built that way. It is, if you like, a plain fact of human nature for Bentham and the elder Mill that we are made to seek pleasure. It's not that Reason recommends pleasure-seeking as the best mode of life. Rather, as Bentham tells us in the very first line of his most important work, "Nature has placed mankind under the governance of two sovereign masters, *pain* and *pleasure*."[20] Such is our lot. And to whatever extent all that we do is shaped by Nature, all that we do bottoms out in the arbitrary facts of human motivational architecture. By Bentham's lights, our ultimate end (happiness) is dictated by facts of sub-rational Nature, and our proximate determinate primary ends are shaped by the causal his-

---

[19] "John Stuart Mill and the Ends of Life," Robert Waley Cohen Memorial Lecture, London, 2 December 1959, reprinted in *J. S. Mill* On Liberty *in Focus*, ed. John Gray and G. W. Smith, (Routledge: London, 1991), p. 135.

[20] *The Principles of Morals and Legislation*, (Hafner Press: New York, 1948), p. 1.

tories of our associative systems. The proximate ends are means to or parts of attaining our ultimate end. Nurture and nature together provide the menu of kinds of objectives we will seek. Nature alone sets us on the trail of pleasure and avoidance of pain. Benthamism about reason in action leaves our primary ends dangling, unsupported by reason and unacceptably arbitrary. The only sense in which happiness, understood as the greatest balance of pleasure over pain, is a non-arbitrary ultimate end for us is that we are naturally inclined to seek pleasure, action-by-action where we expect to find it. That is why Bentham might advocate psycho-pharmaceuticals if you showed him research indicating that widespread administration of such drugs was the fastest, surest way to bring about the greatest balance of pleasure over pain for the greatest number of citizens. Drugging the populace could serve as a candidate measure of social reform on the view. At least, there seems no principled reason why it wouldn't. Because the end itself (pleasure) has no rational support, and the business of leading a clean and sober life is just one means among many to attaining it.

This *arbitrariness problem*, as I will call it, arises for Benthamite utilitarianism with a vengeance because of the crudely instrumentalist character of the view. Notice that the arbitrariness problem, all on its own, is no objection to *any* version of instrumentalism about moral psychology and practical reason. The point that, by the instrumentalist's lights, ultimate ends or basic desires are arbitrary in the sense a-rational is a plain *statement* of the position rather than any ordinary sort of objection to it (whether or not the version of instrumentalism we have before us is a variant of Benthamism). But the arbitrariness problem was felt by the younger Mill, as it has been by many contemporary moral philosophers, to be very serious drawback indeed.

It was, John Stuart Mill thought, a much more serious objection for moral theory than it was for a theory about legislation. Mill thought Bentham a reasonable guide for legislation because the object of law "is not to render people incapable of *desiring* a crime, but to deter them from actually *committing* it" (10: 9), and, by altering the payoff structure, law could serve as a deterrent to agents who would otherwise take actions injurious to the general welfare. The job of the legislator is not to take hold of infants and youth and instill in them such associations as will tend to direct them to seek pleasure from beneficent, honorable action and recoil from the very thought of base, harmful action. The legislator instead frames policy for constituencies whose members may include many men of bad character. As a guide for personal conduct, however, Bentham's theory was weak. In the

Instrumentalism

sphere of morals one wants not merely to alter the payoff structure of actions in prospect, but the tendencies to take pleasure in, or seek pleasure from, morally bad action. And analyzing *these* tendencies adequately requires focusing on more than pleasure and pain in prospect. It requires making a serious study of character.[21]

Rather than fixating upon concrete objectives (actions of various kinds understood as means to pleasure or pain-avoidance), John Stuart Mill came to concentrate upon more enduring motivational forces which gave rise to many and various concrete objectives. These complex states lend order to the subject's objectives *from within*. The kind of alterations in the well-springs of action that the younger Mill looked for in morals could not be accomplished by altering the costs and benefits of actions of various types. It rather required a shift in what he called "character," where the key to character is to be found in these underlying, complex psychological states that lent a kind of unity and coherence to an agent's pursuits. The complex states of mind weren't themselves objectives, exactly. Rather, they controlled the development and direction and changes in objectives under the impact of experience over the course of one's life. Mill wrote:

> [The problem with Bentham is that he has] confounded the principle of Utility with the principle of specific consequences, and has habit-

---

[21] At least, it does in England and most similarly advanced European nations. Mill was prone to see many populations historically subject to direct European colonial or imperial control, and many non-European "races" whose relations to the European races were unstable, as populations whose adults remained juvenile or infantile. For these adults, altering the option space and pay-off structure *could* effect a shift in character by means of legislative or economic provisions. These adults were like children and could have their associative systems altered by paternalist intervention. So, for example, "To civilize a savage, he must be inspired with new wants and desires, even if not of a very elevated kind," and the love of finery could be exploited to induce a newly associated love of labor and economy among the free slaves of Jamaica and Demerara (2: 104). Mill's thoughts on reform in Irish policy are notoriously slippery in this regard, and it does not seem too strong to conclude that the problem with sorting out Irish character had to do with the fact that they were a subject *European* "race." In his recommendations on Irish policy, he makes his focus Irish peasants, notes that they are lazy, reckless, desperate and miserable, but takes these things as the effect of English policy (24: 955-56, 1007). By nature they are Celts, and Celts show no want of industry or providence, hence legislative measures emphasizing land reform could restore the Irish to a state in which they might develop a "race"-appropriate national character. Frenchmen with small land holdings do well, he reasons, and advises: "Give the Irishman 'the secure possession of a bleak rock' or a turf bog, and he too 'will turn it into a garden'" (24: 958).

ually made up his estimation of the approbation or blame due to a particular kind of action, from a calculation solely of the consequences to which that very action, if practised generally, would itself lead. He has largely exemplified, and contributed very widely to diffuse, a tone of thinking, according to which any kind of action or any habit, which in its specific consequences cannot be proved to be necessarily or probably productive of unhappiness to the agent himself or to others, is supposed to be fully justified; and any disapprobation or aversion entertained towards the individual by reason of it, is set down from that time forward as prejudice and superstition. It is not considered (at least, not habitually considered,) whether the act or habit in question, though not in itself necessarily pernicious, may not form part of a *character* essentially pernicious, or at least essentially deficient in some quality entirely conducive to the 'greatest happiness'...When a moralist thus overlooks the relation of an act to a certain state of mind as its cause, and its connexion through that common cause with large classes and groups of actions apparently very little resembling itself, his estimation even of the consequences of the very act itself, is rendered imperfect. For it may be affirmed with few exceptions, that any act whatever has a tendency to fix and perpetuate the state or character of mind in which it has itself originated. And if that important element in the moral relations of the action be not taken into account by the moralist as a cause, neither probably will it be taken into account as a consequence (10: 8).

John Stuart Mill, that is, retains Utility but *rejects* Benthamite consequentialism. In so doing, he rejects crude instrumentalist moral psychology of the sort Bentham relied upon, and likewise rejects the associated crudely calculative view of reason in action. How Mill made this shift away from the utilitarianism of his father and Bentham will be my focus in what follows. As Mill suggests in his criticism of Bentham, the lever he used to pry himself loose from some aspects of Benthamite utilitarianism was itself moral psychological. I will read John Stuart Mill as engaged in an elaborate and subtle attempt to retain commitment to a broadly instrumentalist moral psychology while making room for orderly change in an agent's desires *not* brought about by mere change in the external payoff structure.

Subtler variants of instrumentalism of the kind Mill moved toward focus upon explaining orderly changes in objectives, and stable patterns in human pursuits informed by otherwise various objectives. Such views *still* hold that there are no reasons for primary ends. The psychological and other processes that give rise to complex affective states (those Mill alludes to in mentioning character) are treated as causal processes *rather than* strictly rational processes. As such, any story that can be told about why we pur-

Instrumentalism 39

sue one thing rather than another, or why we tend to favor some kinds of objectives, policies, or practical alternatives over others, will bottom out in a genetic story about how nature or culture, experience or parenting, action or passivity made us be the sorts of creatures who went in for the relevant sorts of objectives. For all that, however, Mill's thought about *sorts* of persons individuated in terms of *patterns* in otherwise disparate actions and objectives which were in turn expressive of temperament signaled an advance over Benthamite moral psychology. For while reason itself still only directs us to pursue one end or another insofar as the end in question is a means to, or part of, attaining some other more primary end on this view, and while the ultimate end is still happiness, the ingredients that go into determining what *sort* of person someone is or could be, the fundamental elements of character, allow for a different sort of intervention into human conduct than the kind at issue in rearranging the payoff structure of actions. In particular, it allows for self-directed experimentation—trial and error research, experiments in living—conducted in order to determine what sort of person one is and what sort of life suits one. It allows that one may rightly conclude that one is a particular sort of person, be dissatisfied with this fact, and set about altering one's character. Finally, it allows one to eschew some courses of action on the grounds that they tend to contribute to unsavory character formations (judgment about character types is subject to two sorts of constraints, one involving ideals, the other involving facts about the person which set limits on how the ideals may be realized or exemplified in his character and conduct), whether or not the actions in question would likely cause unhappiness all on their own. So, although it remains true that if you trace the series of objectives pursued for the sake of attaining further objectives back to the ultimate or primary end in the chain, on Mill's view, and inquire after the grounding for this end, the only answer to your question will be a story about how the agent came to be the sort of creature who would find her happiness in that sort of thing, *this* answer is less disturbing than the flatly calculative answer given by Benthamism, and the place of ideals in the improved system allows for a kind of evaluation to enter into practical deliberation that is not considered in plain hedonic calculative reasoning. Because it remains the case that there are no *reasons* for an agent's primary ends on subtle views like John Stuart Mill's, however, the arbitrariness problem continues to haunt subtle instrumentalist moral psychology. How serious a problem the arbitrariness problem is for the younger Mill's moral psychology in particular, and how successful he is in de-clawing it by focusing on a richer account of the sources of rational action, will be my topic.

CHAPTER 3

Means, Ends and Mill

MILL'S FIRST MOMENT OF CRISIS

> I was accustomed to felicitate myself on the certainty of a happy life
> which I enjoyed, through placing my happiness in something durable
> and distant, in which some progress might always be making, while
> it could never be exhausted by complete attainment. This did very
> well for several years...But the time came when I awakened from this
> as from a dream. It was in the autumn of 1826. I was in a dull state
> of nerves, such as everybody is occasionally liable to; unsusceptible to
> enjoyment or pleasurable excitement; one of those moods when what
> is pleasure at other times becomes insipid or indifferent...In this
> frame of mind it occurred to me to put the question directly to
> myself: "Suppose that all your objects in life were realized; that all the
> changes in institutions and opinions which you are looking forward
> to could be completely effected at this very instant: would this be a
> great joy and happiness to you?" And an irrepressible self-conscious-
> ness distinctly answered, "No!" At this my heart sank within me: the
> whole foundation on which my life was constructed fell down. All my
> happiness was to have been found in the continual pursuit of this end.
> The end had ceased to charm, and how could there ever again be any
> interest in the means? (1: 137, 139)

John Stuart Mill was twenty years old when "the whole foundation.. fell
down." In his *Autobiography*, he diagnosed his mental crisis as an unexpect-
ed side-effect of his early education,—a side-effect which undermined the
principles that had guided his teachers. Bentham and James Mill had
taught John Stuart that "we love one thing, and hate another, take pleasure in one sort of action,...pain in another sort, through the clinging of

41

42 *John Stuart Mill's Deliberative Landscape*

pleasurable or painful ideas to those things" (1: 141). And while the younger Mill's teachers had devoted themselves to disciplining his intellect, they "had occupied themselves but superficially with the means of forming and keeping up these salutary associations" (1: 141). His education had provided him with tremendous critical acumen, reformist utilitarian ideals, and "artificial and casual" associations at the core of his system of motivation: "pains and pleasures...forcibly associated with things [but] not connected with them by any natural tie" (1: 141). He wrote:

> My education...had failed to create...feelings in sufficient strength to resist the dissolving influence of analysis, while the whole course of my intellectual cultivation had made precocious and premature analysis the inveterate habit of mind. I was thus, as I said to myself, left stranded at the commencement of my voyage, with a well equipped ship and a rudder, but no sail; without any real desire for the ends which I had been so carefully fitted out to work for: no delight in virtue, or the general good, but also just as little in anything else (1:143).

And so he drifted. He didn't allow his mental crisis to interfere with his work, and, apparently, no one else noticed it.[1] He completed his ordinary tasks "mechanically," and was capable of doing so because he "had been so drilled in a certain sort of mental exercise that [he] could still carry it on when all the spirit had gone out of it" (1: 143). He studied. He addressed the debating society. He discharged his duties at the Examiner's Office. He read. He wrote. But he didn't think he could stand to go on living as he was for more than a year, and so he made of his problem a case study in moral psychology.

Brooding over his situation, trying to discern what had gone wrong, he became convinced that "the internal culture of the individual" (by which he meant the *joint* cultivation of intellect and feeling) was "among the prime necessities of human well-being," and that he hadn't received an adequate sentimental education (1: 147). Further, and perhaps more seriously, he discovered that:

> The enjoyments of life...are sufficient to make it a pleasant thing, when they are taken *en passant*, without being made a principal

---

[1] Both Alexander Bain and Leslie Stephen give lists of Mill's activities during the critical period. The lists are impressive. Bain and Stephen believed that the whole of Mill's problem could be attributed to overwork. See Bain, *John Stuart Mill*, (Longmans, Green and Co.: London, 1882), pp. 31-32; Stephen, *The English Utilitarians*, vol. III, (Augustus M. Kelley Publishers: New York, 1900/1968), pp. 23-25.

Means, Ends and Mill 43

> object. Once make them so, and they are immediately felt to be insufficient. They will not bear scrutinizing examination...The only chance is to treat, not happiness, but some end external to it, as the purpose of life (1: 147).

Not only had he been mistaken in thinking that the ends he had been trained to pursue would bring him happiness, he had been wrong about the nature of reasons for action. Happiness (understood as pleasure and the avoidance of pain) was so general an end that it had seemed like the sort of thing at which everyone aimed. It had looked like both the ultimate *and* the proximate end of human activities. But if pleasure couldn't always serve as a direct, proximate end of action, and if happiness was just the greatest balance of pleasure over pain, then happiness couldn't anchor action in the way Mill had thought that it did, and it must rather be the case that people were taking their pleasures in passing and aiming elsewhere.[2] What kind of constraints, if any, were there on the ends of human action? could ends be given any support beyond the arbitrary clinging of feeling to thought? and on what basis could Mill himself find *both* a new source of motivation and a different account of the way in which ends "external" to happiness lent a sense of meaning to life?

How Mill's Crisis Embodies the Arbitrariness Problem

Mill's early moral psychology was, in the sense I discussed in the last chapter, instrumentalist. It was based in a conception of the human mind as having a realm of intellect, and a realm of feeling and the thought that, ordinarily, ends sprang from feelings which had become associated with thoughts about things, actions and states of affairs, and how one could shape or alter them by one's actions. The feelings supplied pains to avoid and pleasures to pursue, and intellect provided useful information for a practical life filled with such pursuits and avoidances. The two realms were taken to be largely distinct. The associations between them obeyed some general and abstract causal laws, but, the specific detail of anyone's system

---

[2] This insight formed the initial core of the line of criticism against Bentham. Mill argued that Bentham was overly inclined to see action as springing from determinations "by pains and pleasures in prospect, pains and pleasures to which we look forward as the consequences of our acts" (10: 12). We do not calculate in the manner suggested by Bentham, and our actions often are aimed at things which we take to be ends in themselves, rather than means to pleasure or the avoidance of pain. Indeed, Mill argued, Bentham's table of motives was wrong in its very conception, since the objects of our direct interest determine the content of our motives, and "motives are innumerable" (10: 13).

44 *John Stuart Mill's Deliberative Landscape*

of motivating associations depended, causally, on the contingent detail of his experience and the way in which he happened to be brought up. People basically were stuck with the system of associations that had been formed in them from infancy onward. For this reason, when Mill's system crumbled, "there seemed no power in nature sufficient to begin the formation of [his] character anew" (1: 143).

According to this view, occurrent and prospective pleasures and the avoidance of misery, together with a healthy appreciation of the causal and instrumental connections between happiness or unhappiness, courses of action, and various states of affairs, provided the only sorts of reasons that there were for action. The role of intellect in practical affairs was severely limited. Intellect could discern the relations between causes, effects, means and ends, and so could recommend the adoption of proximate ends, as means to or parts of those ends already given by associations or biological nature. Intellect could not, however, effect change in the system of ends itself. This was because there were no reasons at all underlying the vast majority of a man's proximate primary ends. These were merely means to happiness (understood as consisting in the greatest balance of pleasure over pain), and the explanation for the diversity in human pursuits was just this: people come to associate pleasures with different things.

The analytic habits of mind that were conducive to prudence and clear-sightedness undermined even those ends which one most wanted people to have, because analysis revealed that the best account of the force of those ends lay in the contingent detail of childhood experience. Some people just happen to wind up taking pleasure in the well-being of others, for instance, and so will tend to favor pursuits which further others' interests. One might argue that service to others was good, in the sense that it promoted the general welfare, or yielded the best and most lasting enjoyments, but these arguments, offered up by intellect in the guise of providing reasons for the ends in question, couldn't get anyone who didn't already have the associations in place to serve others, because reasons were only given application in a particular case when the recommended activity already had the force of feeling associated with it, and the attachment of feeling to thoughts was the result of a causal process immune to the influence of intellect. Mill wrote that many social reformers fell into:

> the error of expecting that that the regeneration of mankind...is to be brought about exclusively by the cultivation of what they somewhat loosely term the *reasoning* faculty;...forgetting...that, even supposing perfect knowledge to be attained, no good will come of it, unless the

Means, Ends and Mill 45

ends, to which the means have been pointed out, are first *desired* (1: 375-76)

The associationist account of the motivating force of psychological states was *at the same time* an instrumentalist account of practical reason. Even those ends that were dearest to the utilitarians couldn't be given the support of reason.

Mill thought that ordinary people didn't demand that their associations have the support of reason. They might well demand reasons for actions, but the force of those considerations bottomed out in facts about the natural histories of their associative systems, and in the feelings themselves. Hence, the "artificial and casual" nature of many of the associations that those with lesser analytic abilities than his could rely upon to lend enjoyment, hope or promise to their undertakings. Unfortunately, the trained intellect was prone to reject any accident of personal history as the source of a legitimate and justifiable ground for action, and Mill's intellect had been as thoroughly trained as anyone's.[3] While people with trained intellects tended to require "reasons to justify their feelings," Bentham and James Mill had convinced John Stuart that by and large, there was "no reason for sentiment" (1: 67). He wrote:

> Analytic habits may...strengthen the associations between causes and effects, means and ends, but tend altogether to weaken those which are, to speak familiarly, a *mere* matter of feeling. They are therefore (I thought) favorable to prudence and clear-sightedness, but a perpetual worm at the root of both the passions and of the virtues; and, above all, fearfully undermine all desires, and all pleasures, which are the effects of association, that is, according to the theory I held, all except the purely physical and organic; of the entire insufficiency of which to make life desirable, no one had stronger conviction than I had (1: 143).

---

[3] In the view of some of his contemporaries, and some prominent English intellectuals of the next generation, Mill's intellectual training was itself deficient. Sir Leslie Stephen remarks, for example:

> Mill's training left nothing to be desired as a system of intellectual gymnastics. It was by no means so well calculated to widen the mental horizon...His studies, that is, were more remarkable for intensity than for extent...Therefore, though Mill deserves all the credit which he has received for candour, and was, in fact, most anxious to receive light from the outside, it is not surprising that he will sometimes appear to have been blind to the arguments of familiar thinkers of a different school [*The English Utilitarians*, vol. III, (Augustus M. Kelley Publishers: New York, 1900/1968), pp. 28-29].

Feelings of relief or satiety which attended having come in out of the cold, or having eaten when one was hungry, couldn't be uprooted by the intellect, but this was precisely because these feelings *weren't* the effects of association. A boy flails about when he is in danger of drowning. A girl pulls her hand away from a hot stove. These things are natural. But a man can decide to drown himself when all that he thinks worthwhile in his life is gone, and a woman can refuse to leave the burning building until she has saved her manuscript from the flames. These ends are not "natural," in the relevant sense. They are the kinds of ends which Mill explains as the effect of association, and which the contemporary instrumentalist will describe as arising from a coupling of desire and belief. Where such ends, and the store people set by them, are concerned, we have no reason to expect that we will find perfect accord among healthy human beings. The kinds of ends which we might generally ascribe to the human organism as such will not serve to anchor a wide enough range of human activities to remove the sting of arbitrariness from most of our undertakings viewed from the instrumentalist perspective.[4] As it turned out, "the purely physical and organic" ends were entirely insufficient "to make life desirable." And this insight brought the whole burden of the arbitrariness problem to rest on the younger Mill's shoulders. It's not just that instrumentalism leaves all but the "physical and organic" primary ends unsupported. It's that some of the primary ends which find no mention in biology and organic chemistry texts happen also to be the ends which make human life interesting.

Happiness understood as the simple sum of pleasures and the relative absence of pain did not provide a naturally stable source of specific ends in anything like the way Bentham had supposed. But, as far as the younger Mill could determine, *nothing else* could provide the required support for the most important primary ends either. And so, while he had plenty of thoughts and still could feel, thought and feeling did not couple in the way required to give him reasons to do the things he was doing.

---

[4] A caveat: if the mode of life of the organism itself is understood in a less modern way, if the natural life of the human organism concerns vastly more than what we would investigate in biology and organic chemistry classes, then one could argue that it was natural for us to seek justice and so on. I am taking it that most contemporary Anglo-American philosophers tend to understand the natural as the topic of biology, chemistry, physics and the like. Not all living Anglo-American philosophers have so limited a view of the natural.

Means, Ends and Mill 47

MILL'S STATE OF MIND

It is important to note that the raw materials of action still were in place for the younger Mill in his time of crisis. The analytic part of his intellect, charged with determining means to ends, wasn't in bad shape. He laid much of the blame for his troubles at the door of the tremendous health of this part of his intellect. Nor was his problem, strictly, a lack of feeling. He described himself as having had a sense of "oppression," "irremediable wretchedness," and "gloom" (1: 145), and calls the worst period of his crisis, "the dry heavy dejection of the melancholy winter of 1826-27" (1: 143). Furthermore, describing the initial (and worst) period of his crisis, he wrote:

> In vain I sought relief from my favorite books; those memorials of past nobleness and greatness from which I had always hitherto drawn strength and animation. I read them now without feeling, or with the accustomed feeling *minus* all its charm (1: 139).[5]

While these might not have been pleasant feelings, they were, at least, feelings. Further, they were *appropriate* feelings, given his sense of what had happened to him.[6] In fact, while he lacked instrumental reasons to go on living, he had plenty of instrumental reasons not to. Intellectual scrutiny did not undermine the unpleasant feelings associated with discovering that nothing in his life could provide him with happiness. Those unpleasant associations didn't lose their grip when Mill thought about them. If anything, intellectual scrutiny gave him even more cause for alarm, based on his understanding of what it was that he lacked and of how very difficult it would be to get it back again. But surely intellect could have pointed out that Mill had no more reason to despair over the arbitrariness of ends than he had over the fact that he couldn't flap his arms and fly around the room. On the view he had been taught since childhood, proximate ends were rooted the residue of contingent personal history or the effects of organic nature. By their nature, by the nature of the mind, they could not have rational support. Somehow, this thought brought no comfort. The only associations which had force for him were those which advised suicide. Other ideas and feelings, formerly coupled, had become disconnected merely because the coupling had shown itself to be artificial, arbitrary and

---

[5] "Charm" is a technical term which marks whatever it is that allows ideas and feelings to couple and form motivating reasons.

[6] I am grateful to Elijah Millgram for emphasizing this point in conversation with me.

casual. Thus, while he still could act out of habit, he found no reason for doing so.

Mill scarcely noticed that the very fact that his misery increased when he tried to understand its source suggested that the tie between the two mental realms was much closer than he had supposed, but in learning that pleasure could not be the direct object of all his actions, in the course of finding out just how serious his problem was, he learned that Bentham and James Mill had a dreadfully impoverished view about practical reasoning. The view was that all practical reasoning is a matter of hedonic calculation, however indirectly. John Stuart Mill could still do things and plan to them. He just couldn't find any pleasure or relief in his successes, nor did he anticipate any. His skills were learned, and the learning had involved association of pleasure or pain with attaining objectives. But it was as if the positive affective tone had been entirely drained from his pursuits now. And, come to think about it, it had not been the promise of pleasure or relief from pain in prospect that had moved him before. It was rather that he was happy in his activities, or at least content with them, in the past, and was numb to them now. It seemed that there was no longer even a pleasant component in his engagements. In coming to notice *this*, John Stuart Mill came to conclude that his father's account of the mind was not quite right.

Still, James Mill's moral psychology represented the best available attempt at making a science of the mind. And so John Stuart Mill tried to produce an account of the acquisition of new motivation (something of which he was in desperate need) within the basic parameters of instrumentalism-cum-associationism.

RECOVERY

Mill met his crisis and the questions it raised for him with a strong, newly self-reflective, and analytically inclined intellect, and a deep conviction that intellect was of very little help when it came to changing one's ends, since ends arose from a system of associations between thoughts and feelings which dissolved in the face of intellectual scrutiny. While trying to discover a better system for inner cultivation than the arbitrary method of his youth, he began "to find meaning in the things [he] had read...about the importance of poetry and art as instruments of human culture" (1: 147). In the autumn of 1828, as part of this program, he took up Wordsworth's poems, and found in them "the very culture of the feelings" he'd been looking for.

Means, Ends and Mill 49

In attempting to articulate how exactly Wordsworth's poems helped him, Mill altered his conception of the sentiments and their relation to the good.[7] But he tried to do this without entirely separating himself from the style of moral psychological theory he had learned at his father's knee.

When Mill discovered that the coupling of thought and feeling at the core of his system of motivations rested in "artificial and casual" associations, he stumbled over the root of the arbitrariness problem. Instrumentalism requires that reasons for action trace back to primary ends which themselves lack the support of reasons. We might be able to explain how a man got his ends, but after we have discussed the genesis of his interests, there is nothing more to be said for them. The ultimate end, happiness, is that object of desire which does not aim at anything else. Proximate primary ends are means to or parts of attaining the ultimate end. The only account one can offer of the standing of primary ends is genetic—a story about how one wound up with this set rather than some other set. Worse, "there is nothing whatever which may not become an object of desire or dislike by association" (10: 13). It is not as though one could find proper reasons for pursuing some primary ends rather than others, for seeking one's happiness here rather than there. It is not as though one could view one's personal history as inclining one to a particular range of pursuits, independently worthwhile, where the worthiness of the pursuits (and not one's inclination to take them up) was the real, rationally discernible source of their support. At bottom, inclination explains one's primary ends. And, at bottom, inclination is best explained as the result of a confluence of contingencies. This is why, as Mill would put it, intellect is of no use in the cultivation of feeling. In Mill's mental crisis, then, we find an *embodiment* of the arbitrariness problem, and in his struggle to overcome the crisis, a personal war waged against arbitrariness.

In the last chapter, I discussed instrumentalist moral psychology in general. For the remainder of this essay, I will fix my gaze instead on a particular case of it. I will sort through the detail of the case, and how the foundations for action crumbled under its influence. I hope to show in Mill two distinct pictures of the acquisition of ends capable of lending a sense of purpose to one's life (non-arbitrary, proximate ends). In the first, the acquisition of better ends was seen as the result of trial-and-error. One felt unhappy and dissatisfied with one's pursuits. This gave one the desire to do something different. If another course leapt to mind, and upon trying it

---

[7] Mill's diagnosis of his problem, and description of its solution, has been echoed and developed recently in an elegant essay by Elizabeth Anderson. See Anderson, "John Stuart Mill and Experiments in Living," *Ethics* 102: 4-26.

out, one felt better satisfied with life, then that was the end of it. But if another course did not leap to mind, or if one's first attempts at change didn't hold interest long, then there was a failure of fit between one's pursuits and one's underlying system of natural "passive susceptibilities." One tried to find more suitable pursuits. With luck, one found them.

It is to Mill's credit that he struggled to give a merely causal account of this process. Wanting to do something different, to change *something* about oneself, is not an end which will support instrumental justificatory chains. It cannot support instrumental justificatory chains because it is too vague, too indeterminate, for the task. Making a related point, Henry Richardson imagines a character, Charlene, who seeks professional success. Richardson writes:

> Even if she wants to deliberate by determining what would maximize her chances of professional success, undifferentiated as to profession, she will have to articulate and define what she means by professional success so as to make the comparisons needed. She will need some basis for determining what *counts* as 'professional success' in each of the varied professions, and to what degree.[8]

Compared to wanting to change *something* about one's temperament or character, wanting to maximize one's chances of professional success is already a fairly *tight* end-specification. Still not tight enough however, Richardson argues, to fully ground instrumental justificatory chains. Had Mill given in to the temptation to conceive the process of altering his character as a kind of instrumental deliberation (or had he treated the relation between the desire for change and the result of one's efforts to change as a species of the means-end relation), then he would have violated his own philosophical scruples.

The first account of the acquisition of better primary ends underlies much in Mill's writings on literature, and represents his best attempt to explain how poetry helped him through his mental crisis. In the second account, the acquisition of ends that lent a sense of purpose was understood as the effect of the development of a strong or confirmed character. This was the account that was operative in some of Mill's remarks about "self-culture," "individuality," and "cultivation" of feelings and intellect.

Since Mill thought that character was no more than the structured, systematic, and enduring form of one's pleasurable and painful associations, the residue of action, education and experience, he thought that the development of one's character could adequately be explained and understood as

---

[8] *Practical Reasoning About Final Ends*, (Cambridge University Press: Cambridge, 1997), p. 75.

Means, Ends and Mill 51

the development of a tighter motivational set. The two accounts seemed to run parallel given Mill's brand of instrumentalist moral psychology. I will argue that the two accounts are, in fact, very different, and the first account rests upon the invocation of a peculiar sort of association that it cannot explain.

The rest of this chapter will be devoted to setting some of Mill's remarks about his recovery, and an argument from *On Liberty* in a straightforwardly instrumentalist context. In the next chapter, I will take up Mill's recovery in detail, and trace the revisions he made to associationist psychology in the course of formulating a psychological view that could account for what had happened to him.

THE INSTRUMENTALIST AND THE ARBITRARINESS PROBLEM

The instrumentalism in Mill's first account of how poetry helped him to recover comes into relief if we juxtapose Mill's story about reading Wordsworth with a story Peter Railton tells in a recent essay about how an instrumentalist can be a moral realist.[9] A moral realist has to be able to see *some* ends (those favored by morality) as intrinsically worthy of pursuit. An instrumentalist has to be able to see *all* ends as products of something on the order of organic need or of desire. Squaring the two commitments will usually require finding some non-rational stabilizing source for the ends of morality, and some a-rational process by which a person's ends might come to conform with the demands of morality. Nature is a popular place to hunt for both. If the ends favored by morality are in accord with our natures, if our natures determine that some pursuits are better than others for us, and if our natures likewise equip us to hit upon those pursuits in a non-arbitrary way (perhaps because natural facts constrain processes of end-development), then nature melds instrumentalism with the demands of morality. Railton's attempt to square moral realism with instrumentalism about practical reason bears striking similarity to Mill's attempt (more than a century before) to account for how poetry had been vital to curing his youthful mental crisis. Railton's effort is rather less nuanced than Mill's, however.

Railton works by means of an example:

> Lonnie, a traveler in a foreign country, is feeling miserable. He very much wants to overcome his malaise and to settle his stomach, and finds he has a craving for the familiar: a tall glass of milk.[10]

---

[9] See Railton, "Moral Realism," *The Philosophical Review* 1986 (April): 163-207.
[10] "Moral Realism," *The Philosophical Review* 1986 (April): 174.

Mill, recall, had also tried familiar sources of relief:

> In vain I sought relief from my favorite books; those memorials of past nobleness and greatness from which I had always hitherto drawn strength and animation (1: 139).

Like Mill, Lonnie is disappointed: "what is wrong with Lonnie, in addition to homesickness, is dehydration, a common affliction of tourists, but not one often detectable from introspective evidence."[11] Drinking milk exacerbates Lonnie's dehydration. Feeling worse, he catches sight of a '7-Up' sign, and cheered by another reminder of home, he buys some 7-Up, drinks it, and begins to feel better.

Mill had come upon Wordsworth by accident as well:

> I took up the collection of his poems from curiosity, with no expectation of mental relief from it, though I had before resorted to poetry with that hope. In the worst period of my depression I had read through the whole of Byron (then new to me) to try whether a poet, whose peculiar department was supposed to be the intenser feelings, could rouse any feeling in me. As might be expected, I got no good from this reading, but the reverse. The poet's state of mind was too like my own. His was the lament of a man who had worn out all pleasures, and who seemed to think that life, to all who possess the good things of it, must necessarily be the vapid uninteresting thing which I found it (1: 149, 151).

Byron was useless to Mill because the listlessness and jadedness of Byron matched Mill's own disenchantment.[12] Milk was useless to Lonnie because his real problem was dehydration and milk reinforces the conditions which conduce to dehydration. The prick of curiosity that led Mill to try a bit of Wordsworth functions rather like the comforting familiarity that leads Lonnie to try 7-Up. Much to Mill's surprise, Wordsworth helped:

> I had looked into *The Excursion* two or three years before, and found little in it; and should probably have found as little, had I read it this time. But the miscellaneous poems in the two-volume [*Lyrical Ballads*] edition of 1815...proved to be the precise thing for my mental wants at that particular juncture (1:151).

---

[11] "Moral Realism," *The Philosophical Review* 1986 (April): 174.

[12] Compare: in his notes for an 1829 debate on Wordsworth and Byron, Mill writes: "There remains then, as the only feeling which Byron has painted with any depth, the feeling if dissatisfaction with life and all which is in it: which feeling he has painted in a great variety of forms...[most interestingly, in *Lara, Manfred*, and *Cain*]. And only those who are or have been in this unhappy state of mind can thoroughly sympathize in or understand these poems" (24: 439).

Means, Ends and Mill

And so, just as Lonnie craves more 7-Up, Mill craves more Wordsworth.

Railton postulates the existence of a "wants/interests mechanism" to explain how one's inclinations can come into line with one's objective, real interests:

> In virtue of the correlation to be expected between acting upon motives that congrue with one's [objective] interests and achieving a degree of satisfaction or avoiding a degree of distress, one's objective interests may...play a role in the *evolution* of one's desires. Consider what I will call the *wants/interests mechanism*, which permits individuals to achieve selfconscious and unselfconscious learning about their interests through experience. In the simplest sorts of cases, trial and error leads to the selective retention of wants that are satisfiable and lead to satisfactory results for the agent.[13]

As a result of drinking 7-Up, Lonnie eventually forms a desire to drink abundant clear fluids when he is traveling. Railton (plausibly) reads in this the traces of evolutionary history:

> Humans are creatures motivated primarily by wants rather than instincts. If such creatures were unable through experience to conform their wants to their essential interests—perhaps because they were no more likely to experience positive internal states when their essential interests are met than when they are not—we could not expect long or fruitful futures for them.[14]

The attractiveness of the Lonnie example and the evolutionary story about why it works is just this: it is precisely in matters of health that one supposes that there must be something on the order of a wants/interests mechanism, however liable it is to be derailed by other processes. But *this* sort of wants/interests mechanism belongs to the same sphere as did Mill's physical and organic inclinations, that is, the motives which are *not* effects of association. Railton hopes to extend his account to the other sort of motive, the sort Mill treats as an effect of association, straightforwardly. Railton writes:

> Thus far the argument has concerned only those objective interests that might be classified as needs, but the wants/interests mechanism can operate with respect to any interest—even interests related to an individual's particular aptitudes or social role—whose frustration is attended even indirectly by consciously or unconsciously unsatisfactory results for him... For example, the experience of taking courses in both mathematics and philosophy may lead an undergraduate who

---

[13] "Moral Realism," *The Philosophical Review* 1986 (April): 179.

[14] "Moral Realism," *The Philosophical Review* 1986 (April): 181.

had thought himself to be cut out to be a mathematician to come to prefer a career in philosophy, which would in fact better suit his aptitudes and attitudes.[15]

And here we must pause.

Railton's explanation of Lonnie's change in tastes respected the limits of instrumental accounts of practical reason. The pattern of instrumentalist justification requires that we ascribe desires in order to ground reason in action, and *fully-informed*-Lonnie's desires are the desires *Lonnie* would have had if his beliefs were accurate. Lonnie didn't know that relieving dehydration was, for him, a primary end, but the end was *in* him, potentially, at least, because he was dehydrated and drinking abundant clear fluids relieves dehydration. The lucky encounter with 7-Up allowed him eventually to aim directly at what it was in his interest to do. But faced with the would-be mathematician's change in aspirations, it is much harder to detect the footprint of our shared evolutionary history. The Lonnie example had these features:

1. there was a discernible physiological reduction basis upon which objective interest in drinking abundant clear fluids "supervened;"
2. the reduction basis was such that objective interest could play an indirect, explanatory role with respect to Lonnie's physical well-being, should he take one kind of action (drinking some 7-Up) rather than another (drinking more milk);
3. Lonnie's objective interests could be attributed to any human being facing similar circumstances, making plausible the thought that evolutionary considerations supported the postulation of the wants/interests mechanism.

None of these has straightforward application to the case of the undergraduate who changes majors. Why would anyone think that there is a class of determinate properties that typify philosophers and suit them to their work, such that philosophy and mathematics can be shown to have *different* reduction bases? The tasks of philosophy are various, after all. One imagines, for instance, that some logicians have more in common with set theorists than they have with ethicists, that some philosophers of science have aptitudes rather like those that make for successful mathematicians and physicists, whereas others have more in common with historians of science than they do with their fellow philosophers of science. In short, the relevant postulated taxonomy of types of intellectuals needed to account for the sense that the undergraduate was naturally better suited to philosophy than mathematics seems to exaggerate the similarities among philosophers

[15] "Moral Realism," *The Philosophical Review* 1986 (April): 182.

Means, Ends and Mill 55

and underestimate the similarities between some philosophers and some mathematicians. But it is these "type-identities" that would give some plausibility to the suggestion that the coed was *really* a philosophical type (*rather than* a mathematical type) of person, and could discover this fact by trial-and-error, just as Lonnie discovered he needed clear fluids by trial-and-error.

It is important to note that simply being able to tell a story about how an undergraduate settles upon philosophy rather than mathematics is not enough to get Railton's account of natural vocational preferences off the ground. One student settles on philosophy rather than mathematics, say, because there is an especially charismatic professor in the philosophy department and the math courses are taught by nervous graduate students. Another settles on philosophy because the lower-division mathematics classes are enormous, the philosophy classes are small, and he is made anxious by crowds. A third who is, say, lonely, notices that, while philosophers are hardly social butterflies, they talk a lot, whereas the mathematicians are very quiet; the literature students are the liveliest of all, but they enjoy so easy an intimacy among themselves that they are frightening; and so our third man decides upon a career in philosophy. Many roads lead to any given profession. It is the merest fantasy to suppose that the kind of species-wide strategy for reproductive success that informs Railton's evolutionary account of the health-related wants/interest mechanism could be extended to account for a wants/interests mechanism that would bring a young man's subjective interest in doing math into line with his *objective* interests in a philosophical career. Even if there is such a thing as a philosopher reduction basis—a set of temperamental and other properties common to practicing philosophers and absent in, say, professional mathematicians—this basis is doubtless established over the course of *doing* philosophy, as anyone in the discipline knows. Think how we cringe reading a statement of purpose in a graduate school application which announces that the applicant learned that he was meant for philosophy when he noticed his world and had a thought about it at the tender age of five or eight or twelve!

The problem of the developing reduction basis is a serious obstacle to Railton's theory. Railton's postulated mechanism and the physiological and psychological bases from which it operates are designed to put desires for determinate proximate ends (e.g., drinking abundant clear fluids, becoming an academic philosopher) *into* a man, as his best potential given the kind of man he is and the kind of circumstances he faces, *before* he knows what kind of man he is and what it will suit him to do. The stability of these is how Railton is able to argue that the person fully informed about his own nature and circumstances would have those desires that he comes to develop through the operation of the wants/interests mechanism. But if the basis for change is vastly less determinate than this, then the hypothetical fully-informed-person will be in no better position than the lost, ignorant, dissatisfied person is to say what ought to be done to improve things. What the fully-informed person could say will be something like this: "Look, if you keep doing math then you may wind up a mathematician, and if you switch to economics, you may wind up an economist, and if you keep at philosophy, you may wind up a philosopher. And if you are focusing on just one of these, then it will probably preclude your finding a home in the other disciplines." In short, if the relevant lower-level aptitudes and susceptibilities are *not* in the man *before* he sets off doing this and that, then he *cannot* be said to have an objective interest in doing what he winds up doing—*B*-ing, say—not even *potentially*, except in *exactly* the same sense that one might say that he has an objective interest in *avoiding* *B*-ing at all costs.

TOLERANCE AND TYPES

Mill comes closest to anticipating Railton's approach to squaring instrumentalism with morality in one of the arguments favoring tolerance and freedom of action in *On Liberty*. Writing in what seems a fairly frankly instrumentalist vein, Mill suggests that each man or woman must be permitted to conduct "experiments in living" in order to find the life best suited to his or her nature, rather than being compelled by law and social pressure to live in accordance with custom. Against custom Mill writes:

> A man cannot get a coat or a pair of boots to fit him, unless they are either made to his measure, or he has a whole warehouseful to choose from: and is it easier to fit him with a life than with a coat, or are human beings more like one another in their whole physical and spiritual conformation than in the shape of their feet?...The same mode of life is a healthy excitement to one, keeping all his faculties of action and enjoyment in their best order, while to another it is a distracting burthen, which suspends or crushes all internal life. Such are the differences among human beings in their sources of pleasure, their susceptibilities of pain, and the operation on them of different physical and moral agencies, that unless there is a corresponding diversity in their modes of life, they [cannot] obtain their fair share of happiness...(18: 270).

Means, Ends and Mill 57

He understands custom as a kind of manual for living, based in the past experience of a people. For Mill, custom contains "evidence of what [other people's] experience has taught *them*" about how human beings ought to live (18: 262). It is a kind of record of the "results" of past "experiments in living," and since we too are human beings, we "should be so taught and trained in youth as to know and benefit by the ascertained results of human experience" (18: 262). But others' experience may have been misinterpreted, or may be "too narrow" to guide our pursuits (18: 262). In either of these cases, custom wouldn't be a suitable guide to our actions. Further, customary modes of life are designed for customary sorts of people who face customary circumstances (18: 262). There is no guarantee that all of us will be customary people, nor that our circumstances will be customary.

Mill here presents himself as recommending no new ends to the audience, but rather as suggesting means by which everyone can discover the sorts of proximate ends she or he already *has* it in her or him to cultivate (made possible and constrained by the pattern of passive susceptibilities that comprise her or his nature). Different varieties of human nature are chiefly interesting insofar as they constrain the range of associations which can motivate those with the relevant kind of nature. The problem with allowing individuals little scope for free action, with requiring that they lead customary lives, is that customary lives won't suit everybody.

Now, it is hard to resist the thought that there are different sorts of people, and unclear why one would want to resist this thought, as far as it goes. But this little thought doesn't help instrumentalist moral psychology find solid, non-arbitrary foundations for action (instrumentalism required considerably more than this thought, since, as I argued in assessing Railton, unless one mysteriously is *born* a certain type of person, one's type is just as arbitrary as one's ends are). Nor will this thought add much to an argument for freedom of action.

Here is how we are supposed to go from the thought about types to a commitment to liberty of action: we don't know in advance what types of people make up our society and which kinds of circumstance members of each type will face; in the absence of knowledge of these facts, we must let our citizens find their natural ends by trial-and-error, hoping that luck will come to their aid as it came to Lonnie's aid when he drank 7-Up on impulse; freedom of action allows people to try and err, try and succeed; and that is why we ought to support freedom of action (we ought to *tolerate* one another's acts because we might benefit from the results of their lifestyle experiments, and because, after all, it takes all kinds). Call this the "argument from ignorance."

58   *John Stuart Mill's Deliberative Landscape*

Obviously, the argument from ignorance takes its force from the claim that we know very little about the natures of our citizens. But surely the most efficient means to improving the state of our knowledge is *not* to let each individual blunder around, hoping to chance upon the appropriate sort of life. Even if our citizens find their way into appropriate lives by this method, they will have used up some considerable portion of their days in the search, and few will have access to the means of communication required to make public the results of their experiments in living. Say that 25% of the population is made up of type B people, 15% of type W people, and 60% of type K people. Surely our psychologists and social scientists could discover this fact, and could work together with vocational counseling and placement agencies (and, perhaps, a dating service), to match citizens to one among a range of right kinds of lifestyles (each citizen might be given a short menu of choices, to account for individual variants within a type). Some control could be exercised over the kinds of "circumstances" members of each type will face. And everyone would be "happier." Indeed, guaranteeing freedom of action seems an altogether inefficient and halting method of improving our lot.

Moreover, the argument from ignorance imagines that we all can be brought around to welcome tokens of many types. But Mill's remarks do little to motivate this presupposition.[16] Mill thought that most people in his audience were intolerant:

> In maintaining [that free scope should be given to varieties of character], the greatest difficulty to be encountered does not lie in the appreciation of means towards an acknowledged end, but in the indifference of persons in general to the end itself (18: 261).

---

[16] Mill tries to encourage his audience to welcome many types of men and women by warning that Europeans otherwise might wind up like Asians, and, more particularly, like Chinese people who "have become stationary—have remained so for thousands of years," and have not "kept themselves steadily at the head of the movement of the world" (18: 273). That is, Mill relies upon his views of national character in trying to move Englishmen to welcome many types of English people. This attempt is of little use. It invokes the desire for progress and the competition to be first among nations, and it may well be that English people want(ed) progress and power, but English people also want(ed) conformity to custom and social harmony (otherwise, Mill would not need to argue with them in print), and if the national character of the English is/was as rigid and conformist as Mill seems to suggest, then it seems likely that the English willingly would risk losing a measure of leadership and progress for the sake of harmony (or else conceive progress as the conversion of other national characters to the English model).

Means, Ends and Mill 59

He is attempting to present himself as supplying an account of superior means which might be taken to attaining the ends associated with general welfare: forcing everyone under the yoke of custom is a less good way than giving free scope for experiments in living if we seek to promote the greatest happiness for the greatest number of our citizens. But if types are largely the result of upbringing and education, then we could rid ourselves of the *need* to cope with very many of them by exerting still more control over early education. If Mill's science of "Ethology" was more advanced, if we found the laws governing the production of "the various types of human nature to be found in the world," and could predict "the particular type of character which would be formed in mankind generally by any assumed set of circumstances," then our best hope of harmonious social life might lay in controlling the proliferation of types, not in encouraging ever greater variations.[17]

In short, the argument from ignorance is a bad argument. It is a bad argument because the conception of the mind in which it is based is too slender a thread on which to hang Mill's moral ambitions.

MILL'S OWN PROBLEM

The problem Mill faced in his mental crisis, and in accounting for his recovery, is at once more interesting and more delicate than Railton's. It is likewise more subtle than some of Mill's own remarks about "experiments in living" might suggest. Mill needed to figure out how to explain a change in motivating associations that *isn't* simply the result of bringing one's desires into alignment with some facts about one's pre-existing nature, but is, for all that, constrained by facts about one's pre-existing nature. Mill does not aim to *conserve* his character and pursue his characteristic ends more single-mindedly (which seems to be the thrust of Railton's problem and of the argument from ignorance in the *Liberty*). Rather, Mill seeks to *alter* his character. The problem of the developing reduction base is a serious obstacle to Railton's account, and opens a kind of loophole in the *Liberty*'s argument from ignorance (why not control the proliferation of types rather than give free rein to individuality?). Things are the other way around when Mill comes to explain how his life became meaningful again in the wake of his mental crisis. Rather than *damaging* Mill's story about the salvational power of poetry, the possibility of systematic, constrained change in one's motivational set is *required* if we are to make sense of that story.

---

[17] The quoted terms and phrases are from (8: 872-73).

60   *John Stuart Mill's Deliberative Landscape*

Here is how Mill describes the way reading Wordsworth's poetry made such change possible:

> In the first place, these poems addressed themselves powerfully to one of the strongest of my pleasurable susceptibilities, the love of rural objects and natural scenery; to which I had been indebted not only for much of the pleasure of my life, but quite recently for relief from one of my longest relapses into depression.[18] In this power of rural beauty over me, there was a foundation laid for taking pleasure in Wordsworth's poetry; the more so, as his scenery lies mostly among mountains which, owing to my early Pyrenean excursion, were my ideal of natural beauty (1:151).

Mill's learned associations of pleasure with natural scenery predisposed him to enjoy Wordsworth's poetry. All on its own, however, this fact was not enough to explain how reading Wordsworth lessened the effects of the mental crisis:

> Wordsworth would never have had any great effect on me, if he had merely placed before me beautiful pictures of natural scenery. Scott does this still better than Wordsworth, and a very second-rate landscape does it more effectually than any poet (1: 151).

What Wordsworth's poems did better than other poetry, or painting, or even real scenes was to provide a kind of model for a different state of mind (the thing that tired Byron could not do). In attaining this new state of mind, in part by following Wordsworth's example, Mill became able to cultivate his feelings.

How, exactly, Wordsworth's poems provided "the very culture of the feelings, which [Mill] was in quest of" (1: 151) remains rather obscure. In the *Autobiography*, Mill first tries to describe the effect that Wordsworth's poems had on him by noting that Wordsworth's poems "expressed…states of feeling, and of thought coloured by feeling, under the excitement of beauty" (1: 151). Wordsworth's poetry, Mill wrote, made him "feel that there was a real, permanent happiness in tranquil contemplation," and planted the fresh associations in ground where "there was nothing to dread from the most confirmed habit of analysis" (1: 153). Mill realized that if he could provide an associationist account of the way that poetry helped him, then he would have succeeded in explaining how one could get intellect-proof motives without relying on intellect for more than he thought intellect could provide. He tried to get such an account by arguing that art engendered associations which were especially suited to develop the feelings, and that different kinds of art were especially appropriate for different kinds of men and women.

---

[18] Mill here alludes to his second mental crisis.

CHAPTER 4

Arts and Minds

EXPLANANDUM

Various things were clear to John Stuart Mill in his time of crisis. The first was that intellect undermined motivation by showing one's pleasures to be groundless. The second was that very few people were bothered by this. Ordinary people seemed to get by just fine on motivational sets that were anything but products of reason. Warm rushes of not especially cogent sentiment, directed by mere force of custom, cant and prejudice, seemed to move many of them from pursuit to pursuit rather nicely. The Benthamite thought that their practical ease arose from psychological mechanisms linking a-rational sentiment to ideas of things that they might do, and which then directed these motivating associations with the aid of coordinated expectations grounded in customary means-end judgments, seemed a plausible account of how average people got by, and of why there was such social order as there was. Mill's intellect made it impossible for him to go about things in the average way. But intellect alone could not provide him with a better way, either. All of these things together suggested (thirdly) that there was something right about the moral psychology of James Mill and Jeremy Bentham. And had John Stuart Mill found nothing that could give him a sense of meaning in his life, this grain of truth might have done him in. But he had learned something else besides. The fourth point to be considered was that it was possible for a man with a highly trained intellect to find modes of feeling that did not fail him. And this meant that there was more to motivation than was dreamed of in his father's philosophy.

The son had no doubt as to the philosophical cause of his malaise.[1] Explaining how he got better was more of a challenge. Meeting the challenge required finding a way of explaining: (a) what his father and Bentham had got right about moral psychology and practical reason, (b) why it had been possible to use poetry-reading to get over the crisis, and (c) how one could enlarge the scope of associationist psychology to account for the power of poetry.

Ordinary people gave every indication of operating in the way that traditional associationism said they did. But what of uncustomary people? What of those who were ill-suited to the common run of things because they couldn't content themselves with customary modes of life? Surely there must be something about their psyches that eluded traditional associationism. But what? As near as I can tell, Mill answered this question by drawing upon the great bifurcation of intellect and affect that formed the skeletal ordering in associationist psychology. Of uncustomary people, Mill decided, some were more emotional than average, others were more intellectual than average, and sometimes, more rarely, a man or woman had *both* a superabundance of intellectual power and a superabundance of strong feeling.[2] And so Mill postulated the existence of different kinds of minds. What his mentors had got right was an account of the motivational set of minds marked by neither very strong feelings nor very strong thoughts. What they had missed was how an unaccustomed mind (his own, for instance) could develop a sound motivational set. Poetry had proved decisive in the culture of his own motivational set, and so he turned to literary theory to account for these things. And it was there that his first taxonomy of kinds of minds appears.

Mill's investigation of different types of imaginative literary representations, and the alignment of these with different kinds of minds, is a kind of explanatory *tour de force* the likes of which one seldom finds in the history of philosophy. Ambitious, implausible and faintly horrifying, it is likewise an interesting moment in the history of aesthetics and the history of psychology. In this chapter, I will read it alongside John Stuart Mill's other

---

[1] Although, as I mentioned at the start of this essay, the psychological causes were doubtless various and may have had much to do with the fact that Mill had been raised for public life in English politics, and found himself suddenly sequestered in the Examiner's Office at East India House instead. Much later, he fought to prevent the transfer of the government of India to the Crown, interestingly. But that is another story.

[2] Harriet Taylor was a person of both inordinate intellect and strong feeling, in Mill's view.

Arts and Minds   63

writings, some of his father's psychology, and bits of the work of another psychologist whom the younger Mill thought was on the right track. In so doing, I will be arguing that understanding Millian associationism is absolutely crucial to understanding other aspects of Millian philosophy. I hope also to show the lengths to which the younger Mill was prepared to go in order to preserve a traditional psychological division between thought and feeling.

In brief, in giving a consistently associationist account of his own change of heart, Mill hypothesized that each kind of mature human being had its own sort of nature. Some types of humans were susceptible to some kinds of art (potentially, at least), and others to others.[3] Exposure to the works of art best suited to one's type should engender motivating associations so irresistible and compelling that there would be something wrong with one who was, by nature, susceptible to the relevant kind of artistic associations but seemed incapable of forming them under the influence of the art in question.[4]

Different imaginative artists, Mill claimed, appealed to different kinds of minds because different artists offered expressions of different states of feeling. If a mind had an affinity for a particular kind of feeling (if, in other words, the mind contained that feeling, or one similar in spirit to it, associated with a kind of impression or idea), it could respond to the work of

[3] Mill devotes himself to works of literature and plays very little attention to non-discursive art forms. He mentions songs, and oral story-telling, but gives no indication that he sees either as interestingly different from printed word-art. It is hard to imagine him having much of interest to say about painting, harder still to think how he might have comprehended sculpture. It appears that he thinks of theater arts as staged stories in fancy dress. His interest is not so much in art as in representations with fairly determinate content, and where an art form resists this sort of analysis, he is content to write as though it did not. There are all kinds of things to complain about in Mill's aesthetics. I will remark upon only a couple of them. It is well to note at the outset, however, that Mill seems to be restricting his attention to people who are both literate and (basically) lettered in developing the core elements of his account of the kinds of people there are, and, beyond this, treating aesthetic sensibilities as something on the order of tastes in reading.

[4] There is a *prima facie* problem with claiming that different types of people naturally are suited to different pursuits (a problem which does not arise for the more general view that *the* human being has certain ends). The problem is that the individuation of types is handled through an ascription of characteristic ends and tendencies to form characteristic ends, and it is not clear how one could be a *defective* token of a particular type by failing to form the relevant sort of ends under the relevant circumstances (it would seem, rather, that one was a token of a *different* type). I will leave this difficulty to one side.

art that was "in keeping with [that] state of human feeling;" one which provided an image "so fitted to [the relevant state of feeling] as to be the embodied symbol of it, and to summon up the state of feeling itself, with a force not to be surpassed by anything but reality" (1: 399). In the summoning-up process, motivating states could become better articulated and even could be altered. This, in turn, was why poetry could help someone like Mill who was in need of a new motivational set. Mill develops the view in his remarks about the effects of literature and how they correspond to "the varieties which difference of nature and of education makes in what may be termed the habitual bond of association" (1: 357).

NARRATIVE ART AND THE INFERIOR MIND: WHAT JAMES MILL AND JEREMY BENTHAM GOT RIGHT

Mill suggested that, in a mind of mediocre intellect and weak feeling which lacks both intellectual training and cultivation of its sentiments,[5] "objects...arrange themselves in the mere casual order in which they have been seen, heard, or otherwise perceived" (1: 357). James Mill had written: "Our ideas spring up, or exist, in the order in which the sensations existed, of which they are copies."[6] Weak-minded people retained this kind of psychological structure. The ordinary person whose motives and actions seemed to lend themselves to Benthamite psychological explanation was, in this sense, weak-minded.

According to James Mill (following the work of earlier associationists and their precursors), one feature important to forming enduring associations is the frequency with which their succession or simultaneity is expe-

---

[5] Throughout what follows, I will try to maintain a distinction in the use of "training" and "cultivation" that is not always present in Mill's text. Trained feelings will be feelings that have become associated with ideas through the instruments of praise and blame, reward and punishment. Cultivated feelings will involve themselves in much more complex associations. By *trained* intellect I will suggest the effects of mental drills and exercises, the kind of thing that happened in Mill's education. By *cultivated* intellect I will mean intellectual powers that shape and are shaped by a more nuanced emotional set. Neither sort of expression seems to me especially apt for anything but getting a grip on the sort of view Mill is trying to develop. Both draw some force from the kind of classism and intra-class snobbery that makes Mill's work on these topics rather disappointing.

[6] James Mill, *Analysis of the Phenomena of the Human Mind*, (Longman's, Green, Reader and Dyer: London, 1825), vol. I, p. 78.

Arts and Minds 65

rienced;[7] another is the vividness of the association.[8] With motivating associations, i.e., volitional mental states, vividness is always and necessarily the result of an association of pleasure or pain with an idea or impression. Where pleasure and pain lend vividness to an associative link, further, the relevant associations of ideas or impressions may have occurred but once and still have all the force and endurance of more frequently experienced associations.[9] In addition to the genetic, chronological structure of an associative system, there is an independent order among objects which can inform the abstract, logical order among ideas. Often it is this abstract order that informs causal judgments relevant to explaining action, since these involve inductive generalizations, and induction always abstracts general features from the particular case. But one can learn how things happen by being taught it directly. One needn't perform the induction oneself in order to have basic practical competency. And so the mere fact that a lot of human experience and a kind of inductive record of that experience leaves traces in the average man's practical facility does not show that the average man himself is a person of cultivated, or even trained, intellect. Mill elsewhere suggests that it is not even enough to credit the average man with knowledge:

> [Even] assuming that the true opinion abides in the mind [that has learnt it in passing or by rote], but abides as a prejudice, a belief independent of, and proof against, argument—this is not the way in which truth ought to be held by a rational being. This is not knowing the truth. Truth, thus held, is but one superstition the more, accidentally clinging to the words which enunciate a truth (18: 244).

John Stuart Mill suggests that the principles of successive and synchronous association, rather than logical relations among thoughts or the abstract, objective order of things, structure relations among mental items in the mediocre mind. The synchronous order of impressions was the "order of simultaneous existence" which, his father thought, corresponded to the order of objects in space; the successive order in impressions, the order "of antecedent and consequent existence," corresponded to the order of objects

---

[7] James Mill, *Analysis of the Phenomena of the Human Mind*, (Longman's, Green, Reader and Dyer: London, 1825), vol. I, pp. 83, 87-88.

[8] James Mill, *Analysis of the Phenomena of the Human Mind*, (Longman's, Green, Reader and Dyer: London, 1825), vol. I, pp. 84-86.

[9] James Mill, *Analysis of the Phenomena of the Human Mind*, (Longman's, Green, Reader and Dyer: London, 1825), vol. I, p. 105.

[10] James Mill, *Analysis of the Phenomena of the Human Mind*, (Longman's, Green, Reader and Dyer: London, 1825), vol. I, p. 53.

in time.[10] An associative system which *retains* its successive and synchronous genetic character, then, will bear the mark of certain contingencies surrounding the detail of its chronological experience of the world. *Where* the mediocre person happened to be, and *when*, determines the associative order of ideas in his or her mind. The associations between such a mind's ideas and pleasures and pains are likewise primitive—feelings of pleasure or pain were either synchronous with, or successive to, the associated ideas and impressions. The motivational sets of people of mediocre intellect and weak feeling are, then, doubly arbitrary. Because their intellects are weak, the order in their minds depends upon the contingent order of their experiences rather than the deliberately cultivated appreciation for (or trained apprehension of) the objective order of things and the abstract order of ideas. Because their feelings are weak, no sudden surges of emotional attachment disrupt the merely contingent order of their experiences by making some associations especially dominant and powerful quite apart from their place in the chronological development of the associative system. When a weak mind has strong feelings, it relies upon habitual modes of successive and synchronous association to cope with the surges. Indeed, the surges themselves are often customary: penny dreadful fear, conventional joys and sorrows in the face of common kinds of events, etc. Mill later describes such people as a hindrance to anything much interesting. What is interesting is the lives and works of uncommon people, people Mill calls "individuals." He laments:

> At present individuals are lost in the crowd. In politics it is almost a triviality to say that public opinion now rules the world. The only power deserving of the name is that of the masses. This is as true in the moral and social relations of private life as in public transactions. Those whose opinions go by the name of public opinion, are not always the same sort of public: in America, they are the whole white population; in England, chiefly the middle class. But they are always a mass, that is to say, collective mediocrity (18: 268).

Minds of the mediocre sort never develop at all, and really *are* stuck with the artificial and casual system of associations which took shape over the course of their early education and subsequent experience. However old a man with a mediocre mind is, if nothing sparks him to change his character, he remains somehow juvenile. Such minds are most at home with narrative art, largely because narrative art is based in the kind of chronological unfolding of events that is isomorphic with the conditions under which all minds take shape early on. Remarking on the childishness of the fans of narrative Mill writes:

Arts and Minds

> At what stage is the passion for a story, for almost any kind of story, the most intense? In childhood...In what stage of the progress of society, again, is story-telling most valued, and the story-teller in greatest request and honour?—In a rude state, like that of the Tartars and Arabs at this day, and of almost all nations in the earliest ages. But in this state of society there is little poetry except ballads, which are mostly narrative, that is, essentially 'stories', and derive their principal interest from the incidents. Considered as poetry, they are of the lowest and most elementary kind: the feelings depicted, or rather indicated, are the simplest our nature has; such joys and griefs as the immediate pressure of some outward event excites in rude minds, which live wholly immersed in outward things, and have never, either from choice or a force they could not resist, turned themselves to the contemplation of the world within (1: 345).[11]

Because such minds do not turn inward, they do not form more complex associative systems. The associations such minds are disposed to make retain their externally-prompted genetic character. Mediocre people are given over to outward things because they rely upon the chronological stream of outward events, and the synchronous and successive orders in objects, to spark associations. The associative trails ignited by outward events are, in turn, simple, and presumably are *experienced* as retaining the distinct components that James Mill discussed in outlining the operation of successive and synchronous association.

And here Mill finds some footing for a diagnosis of the strengths and weaknesses in Benthamite accounts of practical reason: undeveloped people, whose motivating associations do not break free of their genetic, component order, *will* operate as the kind of hedonic calculators that Bentham described and upon which Benthamite consequentialism was based. But not everyone is this sort of person. In a late essay, Mill suggested that Bentham's assumption that all action aims at pleasure or pain exemption *in*

---

[11] Notice: on this account, associations between psychological states come to resemble associations between people, and the states of feelings themselves look like the sorts of things that have national boundaries and histories. This sort of thing shows up in a lot of Mill's political writings as well, and takes its warrant from Mill's associationist picture of character. See, e.g., the defense of despotism for some nations (18: 224), the discussion of national character in "America" (18: 106-115), the essay on the nature of civilization (18: 120-139), and the warning that England could become like China (18: 272-274). In effect, Mill writes into the architecture of the mind patterning principles which form the "reduction bases" of national character. The sort of mind best described by his father's work is the nationally inferior sort. For additional references to Mill's writings that turn on such thoughts, see Chapter Two, fn. 21 above.

prospect might have stemmed from the habits of a mind in some ways undeveloped:

> Bentham's knowledge of human nature is bounded. It is wholly empirical; and the empiricism of one who has had little experience. He had neither internal experience nor external; the quiet, even tenor of his life, and his healthiness of mind, conspired to exclude him from both. He never knew prosperity and adversity, passion nor satiety: he never had even the experiences which sickness gives; he lived from childhood to the age of eighty-five in boyish health. He knew no dejection, no heaviness of heart. He never felt life a sore and a weary burthen. He was a boy to the last. Self-consciousness, that daemon of the men of genius of our time, from Wordsworth to Byron, from Goethe to Chateaubriand, and to which this age owes so much both of its cheerful and its mournful wisdom, never was awakened in him...all the more subtle workings both of the mind upon itself, and of external things upon the mind, escaped him; and no one, probably, who, in a highly instructed age, ever attempted to give a rule to all human conduct, set out with a more limited conception either of the agencies by which human conduct is, or of those by which it *should* be, influenced (10: 92-3).

Inferior minds of the sort exemplified by fortunate adults like Bentham, by children, and by Arabs, Tartars and other subject peoples, can be found at large among Mill's English contemporaries as well. Inferior middle-class people include those (women, presumably) "addicted to novel-reading," and those (men, presumably) "we find perpetually engaged in hunting for excitement without" (1: 345). Such "idle and frivolous" persons might be brought around to profit by reading poetry, but they are not "natural" lovers of it, although "they may fancy themselves so, because they relish novels in verse" (1: 345). It matters very little whether or not the associative links in such minds form a strong and permanent system of tastes and inclinations. They are, for the most part, reactive creatures, and as long as things are going on around them, or as long as they can use fiction and danger in order to conjure events to which they can then respond (if only in imagination), they will keep themselves happily occupied.

Dominant Thoughts, Dominant Feelings What Benthamite Associationism Missed

But what of those with Mill's sort of mind? Here, successive and synchronous associative links are not enough to keep motivation flowing smoothly, as was evidenced by the mental crisis. In the mind of a "man of science...

Arts and Minds 69

or of business, objects group themselves according to the artificial classifications which the understanding has voluntarily made for the convenience of thought or of practice" (1: 357). This latter sort of mind has had intellectual training, and so is able to manifest "unity and consistency of character" under the rule of a "dominant thought" (1: 357). In these minds, the non-contingent, objective order among things and the abstract relations of ideas has *usurped* the contingent order of chronology in shaping psychological life.

Does this mean that mere reason motivates in the mind of a thinking man? Have we left behind all traces of the instrumentalism in associationist psychology? No. It is still the case that the coherence in thought supplied by a dominant idea operates in accordance with motivating associations: that is, with desire and such pleasures and pains as operate with respect to desire. Even for the mind of trained intellect, "Thoughts and images will be linked together, according to the similarity of the feelings which cling to them. A thought will introduce a thought by first introducing a feeling which is allied with it" (1: 357). But in the man of properly *cultivated* intellect, this process becomes inordinately complex.

In amending his father's treatise on psychology John Stuart Mill writes:

> [Considerations about the variety of ideas present or available to a mind] enable us to understand what it is that keeps a train of thought coherent, *i.e.* that maintains it of a given quality, or directs it to a given purpose. The ideas which succeed one another in the mind of a person who is writing a treatise on some subject, or striving to persuade or conciliate a tribunal or a deliberative assembly, are suggested by one another according to the general laws of association. Yet the ideas recalled are not those which would be called up on any common occasions by the same antecedents, but are those only which connect themselves in the writer's or speaker's mind with the end which he is aiming at. The reason is that the various ideas of the train are not solitary in his mind, but there coexists with all of them (in a greater or lesser degree of constancy according to the quality of the mind) the highly interesting idea of the end in view: the presence of this idea causes each of the ideas which pass through his mind while so engaged, to suggest such of the ideas associated with them as are also associated with the idea of the end, and not to suggest those which have no association with it (31: 192-93).

The desire to attain the end is what makes the idea of the end "highly interesting." This interest, in turn, explains how the ideas which come to mind in thinking how to support some conclusion form a cogent, coherent train of thought. What we see writ small in the psyche of the man whose mental energies are devoted to entrepreneurial occupations, research and persuasion we see writ large in the mind of trained intellect. Such minds are wanting in finer feelings. They have intellectual strength without the affective culture found in minds of a more developed sort. Accordingly, if they turn their intellects on their motivational sets they may discover that they are at root bereft of justifiable sentiment and lose their capacity to take pleasure in their thoughts. And this is how all the pleasure can drain from their lives.

Now, strictly, on an associationist view, there is no such thing as strictly justifiable feeling, except in this sense: my pleasure at the thought of attaining an end can at times transfer to my thoughts about taking means to my end, and the feeling can come along as my desire is transferred from end to means. But there *is* such a thing, Mill discovered in his own case, as states of mind immune to the association-dissolving force of analytical thought. The key to understanding such states of mind *can't* be that they have reasoned affective components. The moral psychology with which Mill is working does not allow for reasoned feelings. It must rather be that the pleasures or pains that went into generating the states of mind have become so tightly bound up with a variety of ideational elements that affective and ideational elements have *lost their distinctive character*. This happens when intellectual strength is suffused by cultivated feeling in a way which surpasses the usual associative links. Mill quotes Jean Jacques Séverin de Cardaillac with approval on the topic of how thinking men think beyond the principles of successive and synchronous association:

> On the doctrine of the [traditional associationists], we can explain how a scholar repeats, without hesitation, a lesson he has learned, for all the words are associated in his mind according to the order in which he has studies them; how he demonstrates a geometrical theorem, the parts of which are connected together in the same manner; these and similar reminiscences of simple successions present no difficulties which the common doctrine cannot resolve. But it is impossible, on this doctrine, to explain the rapid and certain movement in thought, which, with a marvelous facility, passes from one order of subjects to another, only to return again to the first; which again clearing, as if in play, immense intervals; which runs over, now in a manifest order, now in a seeming irregularity, all the notions relative to an object, often relative to several, between which no connection could be suspected; and this without hesitation, without uncertainty, without error, as the hand of a skilful musician expatiates over the keys of the most complex organ (31: 193-94).

Arts and Minds

In order to explain the complexity of active thinking, Cardaillac postulates that the associated states involved are not only numerous, but also, more importantly, indistinct:

> this accompaniment of accessory notions, simultaneously suggested with the principal idea, is far from being as vividly and distinctly represented in consciousness as that idea itself; and when these accessories have once been completely blended with the habits of the mind, and its reproductive agency, they at length finally disappear, becoming fused, as it were, in the consciousness of the idea to which they are attached (31: 194).

In short, the ideational and affective components in such states of mind alike have lost their distinctive character.

Volitional states generally have this character in a mind that has advanced beyond primitive associative ordering, Cardaillac suggests, and Mill agrees. The man of mediocre mind and weak feeling is a largely passive product of contingent life circumstances. The thinking man is not. And just as a dominant thought can organize a whole state of mind, so too can a dominant feeling.

Minds with a preponderance of strong feeling can sometimes achieve a "unity of feeling" which acts as "the harmonizing principle which a central idea is to minds of another class" (1: 360). However, such minds are liable to dissolve like "scattered fragments of a mirror; colours brilliant as life, single images without end, but no picture," unless they can be trained to concentrate on the strong "permanent state of feeling" that forms the underlying ground for the thoughts and images "passing through" (1: 360). "Poetic temperament" is of this latter sort (1: 358). Wordsworth did not have a poetic temperament (1: 151-59, 358-61).

Wordsworth's feelings were not especially strong or dominant, and so, "in Wordsworth, the poetry is almost always the mere setting for a thought" (1: 358). Wordsworth's special genius, according to Mill, lay precisely in this unpoetic temperament. The poet was able to select "in preference the strongest feelings, and the thoughts with which most of feeling is naturally or habitually connected" (1:358). The "culture" in Wordsworth's poetry was simultaneously intellectual and sentimental. Wordsworth had precisely formulated thoughts "coloured by" clearly delineated feelings which were "naturally" suited to them (1: 358). Because Mill shared Wordsworth's quiet feeling for the landscape, because Mill also had some sympathy for Wordsworth's thoughts, Mill was able to use Wordsworth's poems to cultivate his own feelings. The poems produced in Mill whole states of mind isomorphic with the poet's.

Narrative artists tell events. Orators sway feeling. Poetry is, in a way, closer to eloquent oration than to narrative, but the way in which poetry acts upon feeling is different:

> Poetry and eloquence are both alike the expression or utterance of feeling. But if we may be excused the antithesis, we should say that eloquence is *heard*, poetry is *over*heard. Eloquence supposes an audience; the peculiarity of poetry appears to us to lie in the poet's utter unconsciousness of a listener. Poetry is feeling, confessing itself to itself in moments of solitude, and embodying itself in symbols, which are the nearest possible representations of the feeling in the exact shape in which it exists in the poet's mind. Eloquence is feeling pouring itself 'out' to other minds, courting their sympathy, or endeavouring to influence their belief, or move them to passion or action (1: 348-49).[12]

Idle and frivolous people are swayed by oration as they are by any congenial external circumstance. In a sense, the narrative art that they love has more of eloquence than poetry in it. Readers of proper poetry instead mimic the poet's state of mind in the very act of coming to understand the verse. And since the states of mind represented in well-made verse are cultivated, harmonious, whole states, reading poetry can bind together the components of the reader's psychology into a unified, fused, blended, indissoluble state of mind. The capacity of a reader to develop whole states of mind reading poetry, then, depended upon the reader having enough of the raw materials of those states in him already. In this way, the reader's nature constrained the potential influence of poetry. But poetry had the power, for all that, to manufacture new motivating associations in the mind of the sympathetic, congenial reader. In this manner, poetry could change a person's character.

Because poetry has this power, it is most profitable to read the poetry of the best states of mind. However, such poetry can only have its good effect if one has something of the high state of mind in one already. In his notes for a debate about the relative merits of Byron and Wordsworth, Mill writes:

> [Most persons] read a writer and the one who moves them the most they pronounce the greatest poet. Therefore as it is in the nature of different minds to be affected with any given emotion by different things, men scarcely ever agree in their criticisms, and men generally despise all poetry but that which is written for and addressed precisely to them (24: 435).

---

[12] Mill charges Bentham with having no "poetical culture," but credits him with eloquence (10: 92).

Arts and Minds 73

Poets depict states of feeling. If one is already disposed to have the state of feeling that animates a poem, one will be moved by the poetry. Reading congenial poetry of this sort is a *conservative* method of reading. Mill hopes for more, for a style of reading that aims to improve and reform the reader's state of mind:

> What I desire is, that men would not take their emotion in the gross, and ascribe it to the poet, but would so far analyse it as to endeavour to find out for how much of it they are indebted to his genius, and how much to the previous state of their own minds...Persons habituated to this exercise, would hesitate to treat as puerile and absurd, what other persons of minds equally cultivated with themselves admire, until they had first considered whether it was not possible that there might be some deficiency in their own minds which prevented them from being affected by poetry of a particular kind: and on the other hand, if on a close examination of that poetry which they most admired, they found that a great part of the effect it produced upon them was the effect of a not very enviable or creditable state of mind in themselves, they would perhaps find some reason for suspecting, that the very cause, which made them so admire, must make them incapable of feeling and appreciating the highest kind of poetry: for the highest kind of poetry is that which is adapted to the highest state of mind (24: 435-46)

The thought was, roughly, this: if it was the case that some artists could ignite fresh motivating associations for a man like Mill, and if these associations seemed to provide compelling reasons for action which didn't appear to have their roots in an artificial whirl of sentiment, then it must have been the case that Mill was a kind of man who couldn't help *but* be moved by the art in question. It wasn't that intellect was playing a substantial role in changing the shape of his feelings. It was that Mill, *at his best and wisest*, was a Wordsworth sort of person. Wordsworth's states of mind were superior to Mill's at the time Mill took up Wordsworth. But some of the images that expressed Wordsworth's state perfectly were elements that corresponded to aspects of Mill's own pattern of passive susceptibilities. This was supposed to explain how it was that Mill suddenly could find himself with reformed motivating associations which didn't dissolve in the face of intellectual scrutiny. He just happened to be built in a way which preserved him from losing his grip on the associations formed under Wordsworth's influence. Happily, Wordsworth's influence was of the higher sort, productive of the most harmonious and best pleasures that a man of cultivated intellect might hope to enjoy:

> I have learned from Wordsworth that it is possible by dwelling on

> certain ideas to keep up a constant freshness in the emotions which objects excite and which else they would cease to excite as we grew older—to connect cheerful and joyous states of mind with almost every object, to make everything speak to us of our own enjoyments or those of other sentient beings, and to multiply ourselves as it were in the enjoyments of other creatures: to make good parts of human nature afford us more pleasure than the bad afford us pain—and to rid ourselves entirely of hatred or scorn for our fellow creatures (24: 441).

In short, Wordsworth taught Mill to stop placing his "happiness in something durable and distant, in which some progress might always be making, while it could never be exhausted by complete attainment" (1: 137). Seeking happiness in the promise of prospective pleasures was all well and good for persons of mediocre intellect and weak feeling who were disposed to move through life pulled along by the promise of future pleasure, or pushed from thing to thing by the pain of current circumstances. But an intellect under (or recognizing the need of) cultivation no longer operated best in terms of pleasure in prospect, because the thinking man was in the process of building associative links which broke free of the contingent order of experience. This liberation, however painful or disorienting it was at first, involved a shift from mere training to genuine self-culture. Mill's recovery marked one such transition. And Mill found that what he needed was not pleasure-in-prospect, but rather the capacity to enjoy the things and people around him, pleasure in the moment, satisfaction in the activity and sociability of daily life. He needed to learn to take his pleasures *in the present* and set his sights on higher things.

THE NEW SCIENCE OF PSYCHOLOGY

The account of character and changes in character that underlies the bulk of John Stuart Mill's work on literary images and his diagnosis of how poetry helped him marks several crucial departures from the moral psychology of James Mill and Bentham. First off, the emphasis on hedonic calculation that marks Bentham's account of pleasure and pain in rational action has been put in its place. Its proper home is in an account of the motivational structure of the inferior mind. It is inapplicable to minds of cultivated feeling, and even to minds of cultivated intellect like John Stuart Mill's. Notice, for example, that the sense in which what Mill does has as its object pleasure and the exemption from pain in prospect has become both complex and attenuated. For, even if his initial spur to change is the psychological version of a chronic, dull ache, relief from the pain *isn't* just sought

Arts and Minds 75

moment-by-moment, action-by-action, but is instead expected as the distant outcome of an extended period of emotional development. Moreover, the pleasure he seeks isn't a future reward for present action. It lies in the ability to enjoy the *present* circumstance while being engaged in pursuing further ends. Rather than being the *point* of reading Wordsworth—the determinate, proximate end of returning to the Lyrical Ballads—the comfort Mill takes in the activity is treated as a *sign* that he is on the right track. What Bentham would have interpreted as Mill's determinate end has become instead a mere indicator of progress. It isn't, for example, that the solution to Mill's problem was to just keep reading Wordsworth, forsaking other activities insofar as it was possible to do so. The trick was to learn from Wordsworth how to enjoy the business of daily life.

Relatedly, notice that the change that is taking place in Mill's recovery is itself interpreted as *constrained* by complex facts about Mill's system of passive susceptibilities, but not entirely *determined* by them. Passive susceptibilities—qualities of something on the order of temperament—are distinct enough to permit a taxonomy of kinds of minds. But simply having a mind of a certain sort does not uniquely determine one to a particular set of proximate primary ends. After all, Wordsworth was also, by these lights, a Wordsworth sort of person. This is how Mill is able to move from a view about the beneficial features of Wordsworth's poetry to claims about *Wordsworth's* mental type. But there was precious little overlap between Wordsworth's principal proximate ends and Mill's at the time of Mill's crisis, and Mill's recovery did *not* involve him in living a more Wordsworth-like life. What Mill did *after* the crisis was instead very like what Mill had done *before* and *during* the crisis. And so the change that Mill is trying to describe is taking place at one remove from the scene of action.

The character of *this* sort of change turns on whatever cluster of complex ideas, impressions and feelings underlies attribution of systematic passive susceptibilities. What Mill gets isn't so much new proximate primary ends (other than those which direct him to read more Wordsworth in order to cultivate his feelings). What he gets is the special pleasure of a harmonious and whole state of mind—a pleasure stemming from cultivated feeling allied to good thoughts—and *this* pleasure lends some savor to life more generally. What is involved in such a mental state?

John Stuart Mill's new motivating states of mind *do not decompose themselves* into the kinds of parts that his father had insisted *must* be there. But the state in which the younger Mill found himself in as a result of reading Wordsworth was only *one* such state. Cardaillac's description of the intellectual's rapid production of a train of thought—the quasi-magical composition of ideas that was analogous to a musical genius playing over the keys of ideational and affective mental elements—depicted another such state. And while Byron and Shelley might not have been to Mill's tastes, they too, presumably, were giving us whole states of mind in verse. The introduction of this new sort of psychological state into associationist moral psychology changes the moral psychological landscape considerably.

Obviously, we are no longer in the world of straightforward calculation about which actions will conduce to a greater balance of pleasure over pain directed by crudely hedonic calculative processes. More importantly, there has been a shift in the status of associative accounts of mental phenomena. James Mill held that complex mental states were *generated by* or *resulted from* simple ideas, sensations and feelings according to principles of successive or synchronous association (where simple ideas were copies of sense impressions), *and* that simple ideas, impressions, pleasures and pains were proper, logically analyzable *parts of* complex mental states. The harmonious, whole state of mind that his son achieved in reading Wordsworth, however, resisted dissolution into its alleged "parts" by analysis. To drop the *genetic* account of such a state would be to drop associationism. John Stuart Mill did not do that. What he did instead was to drop the claim that an indissoluble whole state of mind retained simple ideas and affective states as its integral, component parts. The parts crucial to forming the state of mind, or the predisposition to form it, were *fused* in the state of mind that had "nothing to dread from the most confirmed habit of analysis" (1: 153). The complex state of mind had its *source* in the natural history of one's associative system, but the pleasures, pains, impressions and ideas that made the state possible were no longer separable components *of* the whole state of mind. John Stuart Mill wrote:

> When impressions have been so often experienced in conjunction, that each of them calls up readily and instantaneously the idea of the whole group, those ideas sometimes melt and coalesce into one another, and appear not several but one; in the same manner as when the seven prismatic colours are presented to the eye in rapid succession, the sensation produced is that of white. But as in the last case it is correct to say that the seven colours when they rapidly followed one another *generated* white, but not that they actually *are* white; so it appears to me that the complex idea, formed by the blending together of several simpler ones, should, even when it really appears simple (that is, when the separate elements are not consciously distinguishable in it,) be said to *result from*, or *be generated by*, the simple ideas, not to *consist* of them.. (8: 853-54).

Fred Wilson argues that this shift was crucial for transforming association-

Arts and Minds

ism into the basis for an experimental science of the mind by making it an *empirical* question just what the "parts" of a complex mental state might be, rather than resting with James Mill's dogmatism about the composition of mental states.[13] Wilson writes:

> since the parts of a mental state are no longer literally *in* it, that is, are no longer integrant parts, but are parts only in being *recoverable from the state* by association, there is no requirement that the parts be *like* the state analysed; that is, the state can be qualitatively distinct from its genetic antecedents—which, of course, it is assumed those parts are. Motivational states can thus come to be acquired through a process of learning by association, but can themselves be a form of pleasure qualitatively distinct from its genetic antecedents. Introspective analysis can, moreover, uncover those metaphysical parts without the state being analysed losing its own unique and distinctive character.[14]

On the improved story, the mind, or "character" or "temperament" was understood as an organized grouping of psychological states, the strengths and roles of which determined the type of woman or man with whom one was dealing. The states could be brought to become stronger or weaker, to order and re-order themselves, come into sharper focus, shift and evolve subtly, and even react with each other, melting or fusing or coalescing into brand new kinds of states, when they were excited, called forth, or calmed by imaginative representations which were especially suited to some of them. Some of these states were thought-governed and some were feeling-governed. A "state of feeling" involved (perhaps indefinitely many) feelings associated with (perhaps indefinitely many) thoughts. A train of thought was similarly complex. In any case, while introspective association *from* the whole state can produce a catalogue of ideas and impressions, pleasures and pains, that are involved in the state, and while the state is presumed *caused by* the interaction of these (introspective analysis recovers the associative links through reminiscences upon past acquaintance with like images, experiences and such), the elements recovered by association are no longer distinctive parts of the state itself. The psychological account has changed.

---

[13] See Wilson, *Psychological Analysis and the Philosophy of John Stuart Mill*, (University of Toronto Press: Toronto, 1990), pp. 100-151.
[14] *Psychological Analysis and the Philosophy of John Stuart Mill*, (University of Toronto Press: Toronto, 1990), p. 137.

BEAUTY AND REASON

What of the story about practical reason? Intellect was off-stage in the account of how Wordsworth helped to cure Mill. It wasn't directly effecting alteration of the motivating states. Rather, it was placing art in front of a system of states so that the art could do the work of changing the system. One found oneself with feelings of dissatisfaction about one's character (that is, one was dissatisfied with the habitual associative system underlying one's many proximate ends), which gave intellect the task of securing means to effect a change of character. By using its grasp on the causal laws that regulated sentimental association, intellect could direct the mind to the appropriate works of imaginative art, and then let art engage the mind and effect the desired change. This process was not, strictly, a straightforward process of means-end *reasoning*. The end of changing one's character was too indeterminate to support straightforward means-ends reasoning. But John Stuart Mill's intellect discovered an intact susceptibility to rural scenery when Mill read Wordsworth and felt better. Intellect then could use this susceptibility to maneuver Mill into a position from which Wordsworth's poetry could work its magic.

The structure of Mill's temperament left him susceptible to Wordsworth. Mill didn't know this in advance, of course, but his prior susceptibility regulated and constrained the trial-and-error process by which intellect determined that the *Lyrical Ballads* would get the motivational juices flowing smoothly. The taxonomy of kinds of people upon which Mill relied suggests that, once we have made room for indissoluble states of mind, an indirect, causal, counterfactual-supporting story could be told to provide a consistently associationist and instrumentalist explanation of his change of heart. Indeed, the causal hypothesis about poetic associations is at center stage in some of Mill's literary essays. He writes, for example, "A thought or feeling requires verse for its adequate expression, when in order that it may dart into the soul with the speed of a lightning-flash, the ideas or images that are to convey it require to be pressed closer together than is compatible with the rigid grammatical construction of the prose sentence" (1: 498). One could call the associationist account of modifying motivational sets something like "the mechanics of poetic association" without straying far from the spirit of such remarks. The picture is this: sometimes the temporal gap produced by the need to read a whole sentence in order to get an image or thought is space enough to permit dissolution of a state of mind into its genetic parts. The *compression* of words in verse mirrors the *fusion* of a whole state of mind. Wordsworth's poetry was the art best able

Arts and Minds

to "dart" into the Millian soul and produce a fused and harmonious state of mind.

But Mill thought that art was a general good, and that even the duller sort of people benefited from (narrative) art. What was special about art in general? According to Mill, art had the power to draw attention to especially moving images which were thereby linked to especially important thoughts. Through art, the experience of beauty drew together and harmonized psychological states, producing a whole state of mind. Mill wrote:

> in the case of our feelings of Beauty, and still more, of Sublimity, that the theory which refers their origin mainly to association, is not only not contradictory to facts, but is not even paradoxical. For if our perceptions of beauty and sublimity are of a more imposing character than the feelings ordinarily excited in us by the contemplation of objects, it will be found that the associations which form those impressions are themselves of a peculiarly imposing nature...[Mr. Ruskin shows that] every thing which gives us the emotion of the Beautiful, is expressive and emblematic of one or another of certain lofty or lovely ideas (31: 224).

The experience of beauty just *was* the experience of "lofty" or "lovely" thoughts and feelings fused in images. The work of art produced in the reader, viewer, or hearer a whole state of mind:

> The property which distinguishes every work of genius in poetry and art from incoherency and vain caprice is, that it is *one, harmonious*, and a *whole*: that its parts are connected together as standing in a common relation to some leading and central idea or purpose. This idea or purpose it is not possible to extract from the work by any mechanical rules. To transport ourselves from the point of view of a spectator or reader, to that of the poet or artist himself, and from that central point to look around and see how the details of the work all conspire to the same end, all contribute to body forth the same general conception, is an exercise of the same powers of imagination, abstraction, and discrimination (though in an inferior degree) which would have enabled ourselves to produce the selfsame work (1: 333).

Notice: the impossibility of extracting the dominant idea or purpose from the state signals the impossibility of analyzing the state's integrant parts on the model provided by James Mill. The importance of these unanalyzable states was such that the younger Mill was willing to claim that sensitivity to beauty was prerequisite to having a balanced, cultivated intellect:

> Where the sense of beauty is wanting, or but faint, the understanding must be contracted: there is so much which a person, unfurnished with that sense, will never have observed, to which he will never have

had his attention awakened: there is so much, of the value of which to the human mind he will be an incompetent and will apt to be a prejudiced judge...It is true of this as of all other sensibilities, that without intellect they run wild; but without them, intellect is stunted (1: 376).

Mill's picture of the activity of the sense of beauty is related to his picture of sensory awareness in general. Following his father's treatment of the phenomena, he explains pleasures and pains on the model of colors, tastes, sounds and smells, and special sensitivities to some pleasures or pains after the pattern of especially acute senses. He takes it that we regard pains or pleasures as more "subjective" than colors or smells because sensations of pleasure or pain "are highly interesting to us on their own account," so that "we willingly dwell" upon them, and, when they are sufficiently intense, they "compel us to concentrate our attention on them" (9: 212). With sensations of pleasure or pain, "our attention is naturally given in a greater degree to the sensations themselves, and only in a less degree to that whose existence they are marks of" (9: 212). Pleasures and pains are nevertheless "marks" of external objects, just as colors, tastes and sounds are (9: 212). The sense of beauty is like an especially acute mode of sensory awareness which links many thoughts to many feelings *in* images and yields the special pleasures of a unified state of mind.

WHOLE STATES OF MIND, HIGHER PLEASURES

The pleasure of a whole state of mind is a *higher* sort of pleasure than the component pleasure of successive and synchronous, genetic association. The pleasure of the whole state of mind requires the unified operation of feeling and thought, and so brings together *more* of what a cultivated person has in her. It is no mere response to outward, external stimuli, nor is it any simple result of satisfying the inner press of organic need. It derives its quality from the active union of disparate and numerous psychological elements under the influence of a dominant thought or feeling. Beyond this, however, the wholeness of the whole state of mind consists in its being more than any sum of genetically significant component parts. Mill writes:

the laws of the phenomena of mind are sometimes analogous to mechanical, but sometimes also to chemical laws. When many impressions or ideas are operating in the mind together, there sometimes takes place a process of a similar kind to chemical combination (8: 853).

Whole states of mind are products of mental chemistry. The sorts of states

Arts and Minds 81

accurately analyzed by James Mill are more like products of mechanical association: the genetic elements retain their distinctive character in the associated state. While mechanism might be important in the generation of a whole state of mind, the whole state of mind was no longer a merely mechanical mental phenomenon.

The pleasure of the whole state of mind is, I take it, the kind of pleasure at issue in Mill's famous discussion of higher pleasures in *Utilitarianism*.[15] Mill writes:

> Whoever supposes that this preference [for higher over lower pleasures] takes place at the sacrifice of happiness—that the superior being, in anything like equal circumstances, is not happier than the inferior being—confounds two very different ideas, of happiness, and content. It is indisputable that a being whose capacities of enjoyment are low, has the greatest chance of having them fully satisfied; and a highly-endowed being will always feel that any happiness he can look for, as the world is constituted, is imperfect. But he can learn to bear its imperfections, if they are at all bearable; and they will not make him envy the being who is indeed unconscious of the imperfections, but only because he feels not at all the good which those imperfections qualify. It is better to be a human being dissatisfied than a pig satisfied; better to be Socrates dissatisfied than a fool satisfied (10: 212).

The lower pleasures almost certainly include pleasures associated with satisfying sense appetite. The higher pleasures almost certainly include the kind of pleasure Mill took in reading Wordsworth. That there was such a difference in kind among pleasures, and that the higher were superior was, Mill thought, a fact of experience. He explained:

> If I am asked, what I mean by the difference of quality of pleasures, or what makes one pleasure more valuable than another, merely as a pleasure, except its being greater in amount, then there is but one possible answer. Of two pleasures, if there be one to which all or almost all who have experience of both give a decided preference, irre-

---

[15] For Fred Wilson's treatment of the point that higher pleasures derive from more complex states of mind see, e.g., *Psychological Analysis and the Philosophy of John Stuart Mill*, (University of Toronto Press: Toronto, 1990), pp. 259-63. Wilson does not link the point to explaining how one might judge the comparative value of higher and lower pleasures. I will attempt to motivate such a link in what follows. For a development of a more traditional interpretation of the higher pleasures in *Utilitarianism* (one which does not take into account the changes in associationist doctrine Mill was making), see Roger Crisp, *Mill on Utilitarianism*, (Routledge: London, 1997), pp. 25-44.

82   *John Stuart Mill's Deliberative Landscape*

> spective of any feeling of moral obligation to prefer it, that is the
> more desirable pleasure (10: 211).

While one might occasionally encounter a man who appeared to take the
low road of sensuality having once enjoyed higher things, this anomaly was
to be accounted for by reminding ourselves that:

> Men lose their high aspirations as they lose their intellectual tastes,
> because they have not time or opportunity for indulging them; and
> they addict themselves to inferior pleasures, not because they delib-
> erately prefer them, but because they are either the only ones to
> which they have access, or the only ones which they are any longer
> capable of enjoying (10: 213).

"Intellectual tastes" here ought to be the sorts of things satisfied by whole
states of mind under simultaneous intellectual and sentimental cultivation.
Notice that *affect*, not *intellect*, is the proper home of "taste." If it is possible to have intellectual tastes, then, this must be the result of mental chemistry between the cognitive and affective aspects of the resulting state. It is
on the grounds that experienced judges prefer higher pleasures that Mill
recommends higher pleasures over lower, and rests content with the utilitarian elevation of pleasure into the position of the highest good.

Now, on the face of it, it is hard to get a grip on a standard of *introspective* assessment that will cover either the difference between pleased pigs
and pained people *or* the difference between sad Socrates and glad Fool.
"When I was a pig I pleased myself as a pig, but now I am a man, I have
put away swinish things" seems a bit of a stretch, surely. By the same
token, while Socrates might claim to prefer his own unhappiness to the
gladness of a stupid man, it is hard to know why we would think *Socrates*
in a position to have experienced both and so to render competent judgment on the latter. Nor is it clear why Mill has such confidence that the
satisfaction of sense appetite will always earn low marks in a hedonic ranking performed by those who are both thoughtful and susceptible to the lure
of carnal delight. Even if we find the Millian thought about fools and
philosophers at once plausible and comforting, it is not at all obvious that
it is better to be Socrates dissatisfied than it is, say, to be Sappho enveloped
in rich scent and sweet music, well-caressed by Kleis and fallen back on soft
cushions, a little tipsy, belly full, limbs loosened by love.[16]

But the account of the whole state of mind gives Mill *some* ground for
the strange insistence that experiencers of higher pleasures can pass judg-

---

[16] The allusions are to Willis Barnstone's translations of Sappho. See *Sappho-Poems:
A new translation*, (Sun & Moon Press, Los Angeles: 1998).

Arts and Minds

83

ment on the lower. That account, recall, is in part *genetic*. *Everyone* starts life a primitive hedonic calculator, on this view. It is just that the peoples of subject nations, idle women, adventuresome men, education-starved persons of the laboring classes, and his father's mentor never *leave* this state of development. And so *anyone* who recovers the genetic sources of his whole state of mind by acts of introspective analysis is equipped to judge whether that whole state is preferable to its historical antecedents.[17] This is why, I think, Mill adds and emphasizes introspection in discussing the qualifications of the judges of pleasure:

> the test of quality [of pleasure], and the rule for measuring it against quantity, being the preference felt by those who, in their opportunities of experience, to which must be added their habits of self-consciousness and self-observation, are best furnished with means of comparison (10:214).

With the change in his account of the kinds of psychological states that might contribute to motivation, John Stuart Mill makes room for an altered account of happiness, and, hence, a more subtle understanding of the operation of the principle of Utility in practice. The man who seeks a whole state of mind and a sense of direction seeks an actively cultivated, articulate and accurate conception of where his own happiness can be found. Each kind of man or woman will find his or her happiness in a subtly different sort of life. Bentham and James Mill were wrong about the nature of happiness. A life directed at happiness isn't *always* a life directed, action-by-action, at pleasure in prospect. Happiness sometimes consists in something like the special pleasure of a sense of wholeness and direction. Indeed, the varieties of types of people, and the different qualities of whole states of mind and their distinctive whole pleasures shows that "happiness [is] much too complex and indefinite an end to be sought except through the medium of various secondary ends" (10: 110).[18] Happiness is attained by a man or woman who has found the pursuits best suited to him or her and patterns her or his conduct accordingly. These determinate pursuits

---

[17] To discuss *all* of the morally suspect features of this account, all of the kinds of *ressentiment* that would seem to inform it, and so on, is, of course, well beyond the scope of this essay. My point is rather that the contention about the qualifications of judges of pleasure is *less* groundless than it would appear, given Mill's revision in associationist moral psychology.

[18] Mill's "secondary ends" are what serve as determinate, proximate *primary* ends, in the sense discussed in chapter 1. Happiness remains the ultimate end, but attaining this end consists in attaining many, harmonious proximate ends over the course of one's life, under the governance, ideally, of a whole, cultured mind.

84 *John Stuart Mill's Deliberative Landscape*

form the parts of a complex, whole ultimate end in keeping with a woman or man's nature. Mill reaches this conclusion in part by means of his own experience. Reading Wordsworth helped him find his own natural direction.

In Sum

The joining of thoughts and feelings in the poetic vision of a life of tranquil contemplation is supposed have brought Mill the pleasure of a whole state of mind. The poetic representation of tranquil contemplation of rural life (evocative of images) fuses thoughts and feelings about how one ought to live and brings the special pleasure of a sense of purpose or direction to the daily life one already leads. The trained intellect is "stunted" without a sense of beauty because it cannot fully effect this harmonious fusion of complex thoughts, feelings, and impressions in its understanding of the ends of action without the help of the beautiful. But the capacity to appreciate beauty can help to transform mere intellectual training into *bona fide* intellectual cultivation.

Experience of the beautiful serves to explain how thoughts and feelings can be got to coalesce in sensuous images of how the world is or might be, thereby directing a man's attention to states of affairs and giving him solid primary ends, especially suited to his type, which carry with them a clear sense of how the world must be changed in order to make it suit him better, or how he already is suited to enjoy the way the world is. The solidity of those very ends, the likes of which he might have been pursuing in a state of apathetic malaise previously, is the effect of his having found grounds for his pursuits in the special pleasures of the harmonious mental state. It isn't quite that John Stuart Mill had acquired new reasons for his proximate ends. It is not even that he had found a reason for pursuing those ends because he had *discovered* that such pursuits were constitutive parts of his happiness (in the way that, say, Lonnie learned that drinking abundant clear fluids was prerequisite to feeling well in foreign places). Rather, Mill's mood had improved considerably and he could now enjoy what had formerly merely confirmed him in his "dry heavy dejection" during the "melancholy winter" that followed his moment of crisis (1: 143). He learned to find the constituents of his own best happiness in his ordinary pursuits.

The poet who captured the state of mind Mill found himself in at his time of crisis—in which the "fountains of vanity and ambition seemed to have dried up within [Mill], as completely as those of benevolence" (1:

Arts and Minds

143)—was Coleridge:

> Work without hope draws nectar in a sieve,
> And hope without an object cannot live.[19]

But reading Wordsworth changed all that, among other things, by giving introspection a different role to play than its merely destructive one. Tranquil contemplation is a *non-analytic* introspective process. Mental chemistry happens in part when self-reflective tendencies are allowed to flourish without the violent force of aggressive intellection. How Mill had known to use his intellect formerly was as an argument machine—intellectual prowess was a *means* to attaining various ends which were supposed to bring pleasure through the achievement of benevolent goals or through the sheer gratification that attends winning a point against the opposition. What Mill learned to do instead was take pleasure in thoughts and impressions even before it was clear how they might be used to advance the ends of intellectual or political combat. Thoughts ceased to be merely ammunition and became instead sources of joy.

Through contemplating the suitable artistic image, a man is turned inward and outward at once, his mind takes shape (thoughts and feelings are fused together) and the world presents itself as lively and engaging to the newly whole man . Moreover, the fusion of idea and feeling in the whole state of mind is so perfect that its genetic source can only be recovered by introspective, associative analysis in retrospect, and even after the genetic, metaphysical parts are thereby recovered, the whole state of mind will not dissolve. The whole state of mind doesn't *have* distinct, integrant parts, exactly. It is caused by a combination of ideational and affective elements, but these elements have been fused into a whole by a kind of association more akin to *chemical reaction* than to conjunction and succession, or even synchronicity or simultaneity. Somehow, where Mill's poetic associative states were concerned, the principles of association had done a very special kind of work. And this is how Wordsworth helped the younger Mill.

And so we have had a glance at Mill's account of the saving graces of Wordsworth's poems. It is instrumentalist in both its account of the role of reason in action and its continued insistence that there are no reasons for feelings. It has (or, at any rate, *had*) the ring of science to it, and it formed the core of Mill's literary views. But it revolves around an intimation of a special kind of association which it is painfully ill-equipped to explain.

---

[19] Mill quotes these lines as describing his state of mind (1: 145).

CHAPTER 5

Juice

INTRODUCTORY NOTE

Mill's mental taxonomy and his discussion of whole states of mind are meant to account for the strengths of traditional, instrumentalist and associationist moral psychology, and to repair a kind of gap in the familiar story. The detail of the shift Mill makes in his father's theory of psychology emerges most clearly in the discussion of literary representations and poetic associations. But how, exactly, that account is meant to go remains something of a mystery. Or so I will argue in this chapter.

THE PUZZLE ABOUT POETRY

How, exactly, are we to understand John Stuart Mill's account of the power of poetry in helping him through his mental crisis? He takes it that "noblest end of poetry as an intellectual pursuit" lies in "acting upon the desires and characters of mankind through their emotions, to raise them toward the perfection of their nature" (1: 414). He continues:

> This, like every other adaptation of means to ends, is the work of cultivated reason; and the poet's success in it will be in proportion to the intrinsic value of his thoughts, and to the command which he has acquired over the materials of his imagination, for placing those thoughts in a strong light before the intellect, and impressing them on the feelings (1: 414).

Now, there are, one supposes, all kinds of ways in which thoughts can be "placed in a strong light before the intellect." Sound arguments with the thoughts expressed as conclusions, for instance, can place the thoughts in a

87

strong light. Some kinds of threats, like "You'll never graduate if you don't finish the course," could help an intellect pay more attention to "thoughts" too (in this case, "thoughts" about the course content). But the threat doesn't place the content itself in a "strong light." By the same token, continual praise of the expressions of some "thoughts" might serve to direct one's attention to them, but unless one understands the praise as an indication that the "thoughts" themselves have merit, the praise won't place the content in a strong light. Suppose, for example, that I ask you why you praise my thought and you reply, "Well, I've always admired your pluck, and you worked *awfully* hard to get your idea." At this point, the praise stops being an indicator of intellectual merit and so can't place the content of the "thoughts" in a strong light.

There are, likewise, all kinds of ways in which the feelings can be "impressed." Taking drugs, for instance, can impress the feelings tremendously. Suppose one knows that taking a drug could change the feelings in such a way that melancholy feelings, or weighty, dulling feelings would lose their dominance and strength in the mind, thereby altering the mind's motivational system in favor of greater and more rewarding activity, renewed interest in ends, and so on. Suppose further that the effects of drug-taking were akin to the quasi-chemical account of psychological fusion. Finally, suppose that, in consultation with a psychiatrist, one determines that one could regain one's equanimity and good cheer either by reading poetry or by taking a drug, but that the drug was the surer bet. Given the causal account of cultivation of the feelings, why wouldn't the drug count as a legitimate source of mental culture? Why couldn't the "medicine for [Mill's] state of mind" (1: 151) be *medicine?*[1]

The moral psychology of James Mill and Bentham already told us that there were many "superficial" ways of impressing the feelings, foremost among them "the old familiar instruments, praise and blame, reward and punishment" (1: 141). What we wanted to know was why poetry was superior to these other methods for regulating the system of associations. In the associationist version of Mill's discussion of modifying one's motivational set, it seems as though poetry is just more effective, causally, than praise, blame, reward and punishment for setting up complex, indissoluble salutary associations in an educated mind. If all Mill was after was a way of causally intervening in his own state of mind, however, we might rue the fact that the poor fellow lived before advanced physician-directed psycho-

---

[1] I do not mean to suggest that anti-depressants would not have been in order for young Mill. The question is more like: Why wouldn't chemically-induced timely highs and more balanced lows count as a source of mental culture?

Juice   89

logical chemotherapy was available, but we wouldn't need to pay attention
to the special claims Mill made about the associations produced by poetry.
It is the special claims that lead Mill to write about art as an instrument
for the development of character, not just an instrument for altering the
play of mental states. And these claims about the special value of the associations set up by art are precisely what Mill cannot explain, given the
remaining instrumentalism in his view of the mind. What remains of
instrumentalism in the new account is, of course, the insistent bifurcation
of intellect and affect, thought and feeling.

HABIT AND NATURE

To write that Wordsworth "has feeling enough to form a decent, graceful,
even beautiful decoration to a thought which is in itself interesting and
moving" (1: 359) is not to explain why the thought and the feeling remain
coupled in a way which has "nothing to dread from the most confirmed
habit of analysis" (1: 153), once one has appreciated the thought's decoration. All Mill tells us about poetic associations is that the poet finds feelings and thoughts which are "naturally" or "habitually" tied together (1:
358).

"Habitually" is of no use to us. Presumably, whatever is habitual for a
man or woman will be a function of how he or she learned to associate feelings with thoughts. The arbitrary and casual is made no less so by being
habitually reinforced. Poetry was supposed to allow people whose "habitual" modes of association had failed them to gerrymander a new motivational system from dissatisfaction with the old. It can't be that the power
of poetry for such people could come from reinforcement of habitual patterns of association. This leaves us with "naturally," which is equally prob-
lematic.

If "naturally" is linked with "habitually" in Mill's account of the special value of poetic associations because it means something like "in accordance with the causal laws governing association," then it faces the same
obscurities which plague the use of "habitually" to pick out the special
power of art. But if "naturally" can't be synonymous with "habitually," neither can it indicate the activation of some sort of physical or organic
process. It can't be that the tie between objects and feelings engendered by
poetry is akin to the tie between food and hunger, that, *unlike* the "effects
of association," artistic linkage is "physical and organic" (1: 143). The
power of poetry is supposed to lie in its ability to forge new associative

90   *John Stuart Mill's Deliberative Landscape*

links between thought and feeling. Its effects *are* "effects of association."[2]

It is one thing to treat a developing preference to drink abundant clear fluids when one is dehydrated as natural, quite another to treat preference for Wordsworth over Byron as "natural." Perhaps Mill means to suggest that there is something at once compelling and understandable about poetic associations (as when one might say that it's "only natural" to have certain responses to things), something that allows the aspects of associative states of mind formed under the influence of poetry to stay *fused* even after introspective analysis has revealed their component origins. But this use of "natural"—as a term of praise or excuse—will not make things clearer. Indeed, in later writings, Mill himself criticizes such use of the term "natural":

> the word natural, applied to feelings or conduct, often seems to mean no more than that they are such as are ordinarily found in human beings; as when it is said that a person acted, on some particular occasion, as it was natural to do; or that to be affected in a particular way by some sight , or sound, or thought, or incident in life, is perfectly natural. In [most] senses of the term, the quality called natural is very often confessedly a worse quality than the one contrasted with it; but whenever its being so is not too obvious to be questioned, the idea seems to be entertained that be describing it as natural, something has been said amounting to a considerable presumption in its favor. For my part I can perceive only one sense in which nature, or naturalness, in a human being, are really terms of praise;...namely when used to denote the absence of affectation (10: 400).

Pointing to habit does not dispel the mysterious character of mental fusion. Pointing to nature is likewise unhelpful. But if the compelling and understandable force of the associations is neither the result of nature nor nurture, where is it coming from?

---

[2] In a footnote to his father's psychological writings, John Stuart Mill nearly suggests that artistic associations have an organic basis:

> The susceptibility to the physical pleasures produced by colours and musical sounds, (and by forms if any part of the pleasure they afford is physical), is probably extremely different in different organisations. In natures in which any one of these susceptibilities is faint, more will depend on association (31: 223).

The last sentence seems to suggest that some of the associations connected to beauty mightn't be, strictly speaking, associations, but might rather be on a par with sensual pleasures of the sort Mill calls "lower pleasures" in *Utilitarianism* (10: 210-214). But nowhere else does he suggest that associations formed under the influence of art are not associations proper.

Juice 91

The kind of "naturalness" which Mill thought he'd found through the joining of thought and feeling in beautiful images does not sit easily with the governing tenets of his moral psychology or his account of practical reason (now couched in terms of a deeper and richer picture of happiness than the sort that girded the Benthamite account of hedonic calculation, but still turning on the principle of utility). It violates his psychology by leaving entirely unexplained how there could be a perception of beauty that wasn't at root a habitual or learned association of some pleasurable feeling with a thought in an image. If that's what the perception of beauty amounted to, then it's hard to see why an analytically trained intellect couldn't dissolve that association as easily as it could any other. And even if intellect *couldn't* wrest thought from feeling in such cases, it wouldn't be because the associations in question were not "artificial and casual." It would be because the intellect was *inexperienced* or otherwise *weak*. Mill explains his father's treatment of belief as a matter of indissoluble association thus:

> All our associations of ideas would probably be dissoluble, if experience presented to us the associated facts separate from one another. If we have any associations which are, in practice, indissoluble, it can only be because the conditions of our existence deny to us the experiences which would be capable of dissolving them. What the author of the *Analysis* means by indissoluble associations, are those which we cannot, by any mental effort, at present overcome (31: 161).

But what John Stuart Mill wanted was to explain how to get associations which were *immune* to the dissolving influence of intellectual analysis because they were *no longer* artificial, *not* how one might form artificial associations which magically escaped intellectual dissolution. If "natural" is meant to capture the sense in which poetic associations are indissoluble, then it isn't the naturalness of plain organic nature that Mill is marking with the term.

The contrast to "natural" in his account, recall, is the term "artificial" (1: 141). It was the artifice of his associative system, recall, that brought him to the brink of despair. The charge that his motivating associations were "artificial and casual" was his way of pointing to the arbitrariness problem which haunted his father's moral psychology. And what the son is trying to explain is how his proximate ends lost the sting of arbitrariness under the influence of reading Wordsworth. On the associationist account, it looks as though the sting of arbitrariness was *a bad feeling*, not a concern with the *grounds* of rational action. If removing the sting of arbitrariness is like getting jogged into a good mood while reading beautiful poems, then

92 *John Stuart Mill's Deliberative Landscape*

the concern with the grounds of rational action which left him nearly suicidal isn't *addressed* by reading Wordsworth, it is simply *sidestepped.*

If, on the other hand, thoughts and feelings are in a non-arbitrary relation with one another when one is apprehending beauty, then they are not
simply in habitual or "natural" relation at all. Something quite different is
going on, something which neither rests in an untenable extension of the
scope of physical and organic processes, nor lends itself to the instrumental
conception of the bifurcated psychological roots of rational action in intellect and affect.

HAPPINESS

If there are thoughts which are suited to particular feelings, and feelings
which are suited to particular thoughts, and if this makes room for the possibility that literary representations can engender fresh motivating associations which not only *do*, but *should* resist the force of intellectual scrutiny,
then Mill seems to be suggesting that *ultimate ends can have their reasons too.*
Here's why. Happiness is our ultimate end on this view. Happiness is pleasure and pain-exemption. But what happiness *amounts to* for anyone who has
developed her capacities for thought or feeling is taking her pleasures in
passing while doing what it suits her to do. What it suits her to do is not
what brings her private gain. She may be a deeply dutiful person (as was
Mill). But the pleasure of such a life is not a special, separable end of action.
Rather, it is, Mill insists, taken in passing (1: 147).

The pleasure in the life of a developed person comes *en passant* because
pleasures sometimes attend *present* occupations, rather than being expected
in consequence of them. Pleasure might attend present occupations because
the *circumstances* of action themselves, rather than what we do or what we
get by doing it, are pleasant (as Mill found when he learned "to connect
cheerful and joyous states of mind with almost every object" [24: 441]).
Pleasure might attend present occupations because our pleasures are taken
in doing things but not, necessarily, in having done them.[3] And even pleasure which comes in consequence of attaining some end needn't be a component of attaining that very end. Instead, the pleasure in attainment

---

[3] Mill especially praised Alexander Bain's table of emotions for including emotions
connected with action: "'Besides the pleasures and pains of Exercise, and the gratification of succeeding in an end. with the opposite mortification of missing what is
laboured for, there is in the attitude of *pursuit*, a peculiar state of mind, so far agree-
able in itself, that factitious occupations are instituted to bring it into play'" (quoted by Mill, 11: 363).

Juice 93

might have nothing to do with the specific end attained: the *very same* sort of satisfaction might attend finishing any project *at all*, because enjoyment is being taken in being a productive person rather than an idle or frivolous person.[4]

Happiness still involves the greater balance of pleasure over pain. Mill is still inclined to write about action as though something in the pleasant or painful element is a-rational. But he wavers. Consider, for instance, his discussion of emotions (complex, associative states pertinent to volition), in a review published in the same year as *On Liberty*:

> It is certain that the attempts of the Association psychologists to resolve the emotions by association, have been on the whole the least successful part of their efforts. One fatal imperfection is obvious at first sight: the only part of the phenomenon which their theory explains, is the suggestion of an idea or ideas, either pleasurable or painful—that is, the merely intellectual part of the emotion; while there is evidently in all our emotions an animal part, over and above any which naturally attends on the ideas as considered separately, and which these philosophers have passed over without any attempt at explanation. It is a wholly insufficient account of Fear, for example, to resolve it into the calling up, by association, of the idea of a dreaded evil; since, were this all, the physical manifestations that would follow would be the same kind, in mostly lesser degree, than those which the evil would itself produce if actually experienced; whereas, in truth, they are generically distinct; the screams, groans, contortions, &c., which (for example) intense bodily suffering produces, being altogether different phenomena from the well-known physical effects and manifestations of the passion of terror. It is conceivable that a scientific theory of Fear may one day be constructed...*The proper office of the law of association in connexion with it, is to account for the transfer of passion to objects which do not naturally excite it.* We all know how easily an object may be rendered dreadful by association, as exemplified by the tremendous effect of nurses' stories in generating artificial terrors (9: 361-62; emphasis added).

The "emotional part" of a mental state includes "the pleasure or pain belonging to it;" the "intellectual" aspect of the state is "the knowledge-giving part" in sensation, and the contentful part of an ideational element more generally (24: 214). "Natural" terrors will involve such things as the memory of actual suffering and the idea of its source. But even this is not enough to account for some qualities of the transfer of passion in volition. If, for example, natural fear arises on account of actual trauma and is analyzed as a painful sensation, recalled (i.e., somehow copied or recorded) in

---

[4] Again, see Mill's review of Bain's *Psychology*, (11: 363).

a painful idea, the question arises "why the thought of a pain as future is so much more painful, than the thought of a past pain when detached from all apprehension for the future; why the expectation of an evil is generally so much worse than the remembrance of one" (24: 218). After all, on the associationist account of expectation and memory set out by James Mill, "neither of them is anything but the idea of the pain itself, associated in each case with a series of events which may be intrinsically indifferent" (24: 218). That is, even in the simplest cases of dreading an event which one expects to be a repeat of some past, painful encounter, some aspects of the character of the transfer of pain are left obscure by associationist psychology. And the same will hold for utterly straightforward expectations of "animal" satisfaction: why is it more pleasant to expect warmth when one is about to enter the house, take off one's coat, and settle into a cozy evening than to remember having come in from the cold the night before?

The Transfer Model versus the Magnet and Filter Model

The problem of coping with distinctions between remembered pleasure and expected pleasure might be got around by simply adding an empirical generalization about the asymmetry of prospective and remembered feelings in order to cover the empirical regularity. The other problem Mill gestures toward, however, is *much* more serious. The classical associationists (James Mill, for example, and David Hume) went to great lengths to analyze relations among contentful states (ideas and perceptions, for example). There had been many attempts also to develop elaborate tables of emotions (Mill's remark is drawn from his discussion of Alexander Bain's table of emotions, for instance). But such analyses of emotion as had been thereby provided turned on analyses of their *ideational* components, together, in some cases, with some physiological speculation on their bodily aspects (e.g., notes about the effects of anxiety on the digestion, scattered speculations on the nervous system). The place of pleasure and pain in all of this was rather ambiguous. There was, on the one hand, a tendency to treat pleasure and pain as phenomenal states—feelings on a par with sensations in some ways—and to treat their transfer from object to object as happening alongside the association among ideational contents, as though pleasure and pain might follow the same kinds of trails as thought did. So, for example, if I came to delight in helping others we could explain it by pointing to how I was rewarded for doing so as a child, and punished for refusing to do so. When the ideational content of my motivating association shifted from the pleasure of private gain (rewards) to direct pleasure in

Juice 95

an improvement in others' conditions, the new motive could be analyzed as different in its *object* from the earlier motive (I sought rewards for me as a child, I seek others' welfare as an adult), and different in its *species* (my motives were *egoistic* before, and are disinterested now; I am now willing to sacrifice some of my own welfare for the sake of others' interests; my motives now are *benevolent* rather than egoistic). In this way, the pleasures of, e.g., benevolence could be *distinguished* from egoistic pleasures, even though both sorts of pleasure are *mine*.

Some of the speculative physiology seemed to have been in the service of this kind of treatment of pleasure and pain: just as other bodily states underlie and accompany associative processes, so too sensation-like states go along with associations; the sensational component, however, will tend diminish as the associative trail becomes ever more remote from its source, just as memory images of things once seen are less distinct and rich in detail than are immediate visual perceptions. My pleasure in private gain fades. Pleasure now clings immediately to thought of others' well-being, albeit a fainter pleasure than the intenser sort that marked my early moral training.

In this sort of account, notice, *all* of the work of explaining and individuating emotion and motivation is actually done through the analyses of relations among ideational contents. Both the species of motivation and the object of motivation are explained in terms of the content of the ideas involved, not the quality of pleasure.

On the other hand, however, an account which *assumes* transfer of pleasure or pain from impression-to-idea-to-idea (growing weaker as the associative system becomes more complex and less dependent on the detail of its source) couldn't be quite right, because pleasures and pains were *themselves* supposed to explain links between ideational contents. In the first place, ideational contents were, all on their own, often inert. The feelings "clinging" to thoughts provided the habitual associative links between some contents. In the second place, some trains of thought involved apparently unrelated contents being brought into *new* and striking relations. Recall Mill's comment on cogent, novel thinking:

> the various ideas of the train are not solitary in his mind, but there coexists with all of them...he highly interesting idea of the end in view: the presence of this idea causes each of the ideas which pass through his mind while so engaged, to suggest such of the ideas associated with them as are also associated with the idea of the end, and not to suggest those which have no association with it (31: 193).

The "idea of the end in view" is a motivating association. But the pleasure-in-prospect carried in it does not merely follow along with the train of thought. It *draws out* ideational elements pertinent to the thinker's end, and, somehow, the quality of excitation in the system is supposed to act both as a *magnet* for potentially relevant ideas and a *filter* for useless contents which otherwise might interrupt the flow of thought.

Notice: it *can't* be that the explanation for novel thinking is that "Thoughts and images [are] linked together according to the similarity of the feelings which cling to them" (1: 357). Rather, the end in the service of which one thinks has a feeling clinging to it which brings to the fore similarities in thought that were *nowhere* evident before the new train of thought got going. Else the train of thought would not have its novelty.

According to the associationist story about motivation, the pleasure-in-prospect attached to an end is crucial to explaining why people act (in this case, to explaining why useful thinking happens). But understood as a simple affective accompaniment to contents which become associated over the course of one's experience, a feel-y bit which is itself contentless, it is mysterious why it should have *any* role to play in the explanation of how some ideational components come to be seen as relevant to a train of thought, and it is still more obscure why the pleasant anticipation of providing cogent support for conclusions all by itself should have the capacity to help the mind filter or screen out irrelevant contents. On the face of it, at least, the *only* sort of thing that could do *either sort of work* would *itself* be contentful.

The *idea* of the end is contentful, of course. And what makes it an idea of an *end* (rather than just any old representation of a possible future state of affairs brought about by one's own efforts) is the motivational "juice" supplied by pleasure-in-prospect. So it might be thought that the pleasure clinging to the idea of finding evidential or argumentative support for one's conclusion could explain how the train of thought gets rolling. But merely having an avid interest in getting a good argument for a conclusion is rarely enough all on its own to increase the chances that one will find such an argument. One's desire can keep one hunting for the good argument, and perseverance may help, of course. The intensity of one's attachment to the end may make one crow with victory if one manages to figure things out, or else leave one deeply unhappy if one fails. Nevertheless, wanting to make a good argument is not the same as being equipped to make one.

I rather suspect that things may as easily go otherwise. Sometimes those arguments which compel lasting attention in many of the areas where Mill dug in seem the product of plain fascination with a topic rather than the outcome of wanting to win a point. Sometimes (as seems to have been

Juice 97

the case with Mill), long training in argument leaves one with a kind of compulsion to pursue arguments quite apart from the hope that one is on the verge of a happy victory. Mill's mental crisis may be read, for example, as the outcome of pressing an argument too hard. Pressing on opinions until they no longer can withstand the scrutiny, and then confronting the task of thinking through the wreckage is rarely a moment of unmitigated joy.

What matters for my purposes, however, is just this: on Mill's account, pleasure has both too much work to do and too little work to do. It is over-burdened because it is supposed to explain how habitual modes of thought get going, how relevant content is illuminated in novel thinking, how irrelevant content is suppressed, how superstition and bias hold sway in a mind, and also (although I will not discuss this) irrational psychological processes and volitional perversity. It is woefully under-theorized because the account requires that pleasure all on its own be entirely contentless. It does its work by "clinging" to ideas, not by being an idea. Ideas carry it, are drawn to it, are kept at bay by it. It is like some lovely partner to thoughts for the sake of which ideas move around, order and reorder themselves. While, at the same time, the ideas unaccompanied by pleasure are not supposed to be capable of going through their "motions" at all. In this sense, in light of the kind of gendering of reason and emotion I mentioned in connection with Mill commentary in the first chapter, Mill's story about pleasure reads more like an incoherent romance than the product of an improved analysis of the phenomena of the human mind. The "juice" fuel-ing the engines of thought and action wouldn't seem all on its own to add much to an explanation of either. Rather, the content of thought and of volitional states seems to do the real work. But if we drain off the juice, we are supposed to be left with no changes to explain.

In short, the "transfer of passion to objects which do not naturally excite it" is absolutely crucial not only to the associationist account of voli-tion, but also to the associationist account of thought. And this "transfer" becomes more and more strange the harder one presses the account.

THE PLACE OF PLEASURE AND PAIN

The problem, I take it, is that pleasure and pain are figuring as primitives of some sort in both traditional associationism and Mill's revision. And the primitive character seems to involve the assumption that pleasure and pain are contentless feel-y bits attaching themselves to ideas and impressions. There is the suggestion that, in infancy at least, the principle of attachment

98 *John Stuart Mill's Deliberative Landscape*

is animal: what is physiologically good for the organism is pleasant to it; what is physiologically bad for the organism is painful to it. This has a certain plausibility. But even simple pursuit of pleasure and avoidance of pain in prospect, is, in the mature human, more complex than can be accounted for by *retaining* the a-rational, "natural," feel-y bit understanding of pleasure and pain, and adding that, in us, these feely-bits *attach themselves to ideas by association.* The account sheds *no* light at all, for instance, on the practical difference between expecting and remembering pleasant or painful situations. Relatedly, it cannot account for the difference between memory and expectation on the one hand, acts of imagination which allow "us to conceive the absent as if it were present, the imaginary as if it were real, and to clothe it in the feelings which, if it were indeed real, it would bring along with it," on the other (10: 92). (Neither the past nor the future is present, and the mental representations of the past and of possible futures likewise come "clothed" in "feelings" on the associationist view.) It leaves obscure the relations between the transfer model and the magnet-and-filter model. Worse, it is *wholly* insufficient to account for the role that pleasure is now playing in Mill's enlarged account of happiness.

The enlarged account of happiness is capacious enough to accommodate the fact that the *intrinsically same* kinds of actions, ends, and objects which left Mill cold at the time of his mental crisis become suffused with pleasure through a change in *philosophical perspective* on their significance. What Mill did before the crisis and during the crisis was pretty much the same as what he did after the crisis. This is, one assumes, partly why no one noticed that he was *in* crisis. Virtually nothing about the external conditions of his daily life changed over the course of the crisis. Nothing about his past changed, obviously. And yet he went from feeling that all of his pursuits were groundless to feeling his life supremely grounded and meaningful. Doubtless, *this* shift was good for him, *qua* organism. But the desirability of the shift is not enough to account for his having made it. The shift was partly the result of *rethinking* the nature of happiness and the place of pleasure in explaining rational action.

And here there is a real question about what kind of work pleasure is doing in the account. It might be any of these (I do not mean this list to be exhaustive):

1. Pleasure is both a-rational and free-floating—it simply comes and goes, and there's no guarantee at all *where* it will attach itself (sometimes to thought about attaining proximate ends the ideas of which are pleasant, sometimes to actions themselves, sometimes to any attainment at all, sometimes to the circumstances of

Juice   99

action, sometimes to one's sense of one's own state of mind quite apart from where one is or what one is doing), and although the strength of the pleasant associations exhibits some interesting regularities and asymmetries, the variety of work that pleasure does, together with the variety of ways it can show up, give pleasure the status of unanlyzable, inconstant mental "juice" that is, for all that, crucial to explaining irrational, a-rational, *and* rational mental processes alike; moreover, pleasure plays the same roles in explaining each of the three sorts of processes.

2. The attachment of (a-rational, felt) pleasure to ideas and impressions is governed by many forces, among them, organic processes, habitual reinforcement of learned associations, evaluative judgment about the worthiness of objects to be sources of pleasure (which is what Mill suggests in urging us to immerse ourselves in the work of uncongenial poets should we find that our fondness for the congenial stems from "a not very enviable or creditable state of mind" [26: 436]), the relevance of considerations to a coherent, abstract train of thought, and the contingent order of experience.

3. Pleasures themselves are reflective of, responsive to, and subjects of judgments; the apparent free-floatingness of pleasure isn't a species of psychological volatility or the mobility of a physiological quantity in a system, it rather signals that virtually anything can be made an object of intellectual scrutiny.

If (1) is the case, then it is hard to see how we are going to get an interesting general account of the role of pleasure in practice. One wonders, for example, why one wouldn't just leave pleasure to the side and run the whole account in terms of relations among ideational contents.

Mill seems to hold some version of (2), provisionally at least. But the account he gives of the special importance of art and beauty is pressing toward a version of (3). If we take some version of (3), however, then the soul of happiness has become sensitive to intellect in a way that suggests we might supply *reasons*, not merely cause, for our ultimate end and its constituents.

Mill's happiness, in the wake of his recovery, involved pleasures experienced while performing actions undertaken for the sake of attaining many and various determinate ends (which were themselves fitted to his improved character). His happiness was likewise found through the pleasure he learned to take in the things and people that filled his world, and the pleasure he found in the attainment of some ends. The whole of it was

John Stuart Mill's Deliberative Landscape

now grounded in a more harmonious mental life. The easiest way to account for this glad suffusion of pleasure would be to suggest that, properly, feeling and thought are not so distinct as James Mill and Bentham had supposed. The "artifice" of John Stuart Mill's early training, then, would lie not so much with a failure to *balance* intellectual training with sentimental cultivation, but rather with the calculated (however inadvertent) *production* of a ridiculous and devastating separation of thought and feeling that could not but lead to mental instability, however common such instability might me in some groups of people. I will try to make this point by way of an analogy.

Undetached Mind-Parts[5]

There are several ways to go about the business of strength training in a gym. One involves lifting free weights and manipulating them in order to target and develop various muscle groups. Another involves using weight machines which are constructed in such a way that proper positioning while using the machines automatically results in targeting particular muscle groups. If one uses only machines, the following curious thing happens: one's muscles are strengthened in isolated groups, and the mere fact that one can handle great weights on the machines is no guarantee that one can carry heavy objects up a flight of stairs, or even *lift* heavy objects, without injury. Further, one acquires very little by way of increase in balance or grace no matter how beautifully one has sculpted one's body with the aid of machines. Rather than having a strong body, one has strong, undetached body-parts. If one wants to *do* anything in daily life which requires strength, however, one needs a strong body. In this sense, exclusive concentration on machine-based weight-training offers more by way of aesthetic benefit than it offers by way of an increase in strength.

I would suggest that one way to diagnose the problem with Mill's early mental training is by analogy with machine-based weight-training: rather than leaving him with a strong mind, Mill's "education" left him with some artificially isolated groupings of strong mind-parts. The fact that he could use his training to win arguments in debating society and make incisive criticisms of positions in print ought no more convince us that his mind was strong than the fact that a man can handle massive

---

[5] My use of "undetached" has its source in one of Quine's examples in "Two Dogmas of Empiricism," reprinted in *From a Logical Point of View*, (Harvard University Press: Cambridge, Mass., 1953), pp. 20-46. My use of Quine's picture departs rather significantly from his.

Juice

weights on a machine ought to convince us that he has a strong body.

Of course, no amount of intellectual drilling seems capable of effecting as perfect an isolation of "parts" as well-designed weight machines do. The pervasiveness of "feeling" in the associationist account of thought seems somehow to register this much: every time the associationist goes to discuss how thinking happens, feeling is implicated. Likewise, the tendency to individuate "feelings" in terms of the ideational contents to which they "cling" suggests that the two are not so distinct as associationism suggests: pleasure never shows up all on its own in the account of thought or volition, but instead comes packaged up with content. Notice that the multiplication of obscurities in both sorts of story seems above all the result of an attempt to treat separately two aspects of psychological functioning which cannot be entirely separated. Nothing happens without both idea and affect, but how the two interact is largely inexplicable, given the bifurcation of thought and feeling. Drop that bifurcation, however, and you undermine both the picture of the psychological antecedents of action and the instrumentalist strain that plays out in this sort of moral psychology by allowing the inter-penetration of reason and passion, intellect and affect, thought and feeling.

If happiness consists in the greatest balance of pleasure over pain, for instance, and if pleasure (at least) has something of reason in it, then there could well be reasons for pursuing what Mill takes to be the ultimate end in human life. Mill at (what I take to be) his best moves in precisely this direction. He never quite arrives at what would look to be his destination (ridding himself of the cumbersome instrumentalist remains of associationism). But he comes very close.

Basically, Mill struggled to describe a relation between thought and feeling which cannot be made to fit his picture of the mind and his conception of the role of reason in practice. Either the story about the power of associations formed under the influence of beauty is wrong (in which case, all of the arbitrariness that left Mill in a state of mental crisis comes rushing back in), or else such associations do indeed resist the damaging effects of analysis precisely because they *aren't* the sorts of things you can account for in moral psychology rooted in the instrumentalist separation of thought and feeling.

Oddly enough, Mill sensed this. Intimations of a very different moral psychology are in the offing in his writings on art, and underlie many of his remarks on character and individuality. He never quite broke away from instrumentalist moral psychology, but it's hard to read him without feeling him strain against the limits of those views. In the next chapter, I will again take up Mill's arguments for freedom of action in *On Liberty*, this time leaving the argument from ignorance behind rather quickly.

CHAPTER 6

Liberty, Ideals and Moral Nature

On Liberty

> The object of this Essay is to assert one very simple principle, as enti-
> tled to govern absolutely the dealings of society with the individual
> in the way of compulsion and control, whether the means used is
> physical force in the form of legal penalties. or the moral coercion of
> public opinion. That principle is, that the sole end for which
> mankind are warranted, individually or collectively, in interfering
> with the liberty of action of their number is self-protection. That the
> only purpose for which power can be rightfully exercised over any
> member of a civilized community, against his will, is to prevent harm
> to others. His own good, either physical or moral, is not a sufficient
> warrant (18: 223).

On Liberty may be John Stuart Mill's best known book. It may also be the
best loved book in a liberal tradition that the essay helped both to articulate and to redirect. In it, Mill provides a utilitarian defense of the liberty
principle. The kind of utilitarianism in question here is not Benthamite
consequentialism, but rather the sort that aims at the greatest happiness
(broadly construed) for the greatest number in the sense operative in his
discussion of the higher pleasures: happiness in living, where the best happiness draws in the pleasures of cultivated whole states of mind, rather than
happiness understood as a quantity of pleasure aimed at in consequence of
doing this or that. Mill recognizes that substantial protections from interference may not seem the most direct or best policy for promoting happiness in any sense, but argues that the alternative—allowing a stultifying
new orthodoxy to take shape in Victorian England and crush individuali-

ty—is a real danger and one that utilitarians and other liberals must fight against.

Mill thought that his essay on liberty would outlive most of his other writings, in part because it was his joint production with Harriet Taylor, and in part because the turmoil of modern society would bring out in ever greater relief "the importance, to man and society, of a large variety in types of character, and of giving full freedom to human nature to expand itself in innumerable and conflicting directions" (1: 259).

The essay met with mixed critical reception. Some reviewers were plainly baffled at the suggestion that there was any danger at all that the florid proliferation of opinion and unconventional lifestyles that they saw around them might give way to a new orthodoxy.[1] Since John Stuart Mill and Harriet Taylor had spent twenty-three years of their association in some peril of losing everything because their intimacy was unconventional, and had managed to preserve their relations only at considerable cost to themselves, they were, perhaps, more sensitive to the power of customary opinion than were some of the critics. Interestingly, Robert Bell, writing for the *Westminster Review*, connected Mill's warnings to dangers which attended the current run of Protestant thought and practice,[2] which were one of the sources of trouble for Mill and Harriet.

Other readers took it that Mill's views were outright radical. These were the critics who *rightly* surmised that Mill's condemnation of custom involved an assault on the institutions of marriage and family life (Mill thought marriage contracts to require the near enslavement of married women in practice), and so on the social order that set the terms for the private lives of the essay's audience.[3] Properly read, among other things, the *Liberty* provides an argument in support of a massive (if measured and carefully balanced) transformation in the formal institutions of intimacy, enshrined in law and patrolled variously through the grand aggregation of social penalties made possible through informal gossip-mongering, networks of private influence, status and reputation, scandal and censure focused upon what Mill took to be matters where the individual was sovereign. That the force of his remarks went unnoticed by some readers is no reason to suppose that the essay had no very great implications for thought and practice. That many of his readers were perfectly content with the existing order of custom in private life did not mean that custom was not a force for stagnation and mediocrity, either, or so Mill would argue, at any rate.

MacKenzie was probably right in claiming that Mill simply argues that:

in matters in which the conduct of A need not hurt B or C, unless they like, there should be perfect freedom, legal and social, to do the act and stand the consequences, that this does not justify the infliction by society of penal 'consequences'...such as would be justly applicable to conduct which was *intended* by A to be injurious to C and D, or which must inevitably and beyond dispute be so to them or others...It will be observed that by this hypothesis the ground taken up by A is open ground. He may be wrong: B and C and all the rest may think him so, and they are entitled to exhibit their view of the matter both to A and among themselves. Of course, too, as no one is bound to take any one else as a friend or acquaintance, C and D are entitled to avoid B; but, adds Mr. Mill, with his usual delicacy of conscience, 'not to parade the avoidance'—which would be inflicting an injury...—all he contends is that new opinion should have a fair hearing, and new conduct fair handling.[4]

But, however unobjectionable this view might sound, MacKenzie was, I think, also right to argue that it was then (and, I suspect, still is) so far from being realized in practice as to count as a radical position on freedom of action. Mill defends liberty of thought and discussion in Chapter Two of his essay. The defense of freedom of action is given in Chapter Three, "Of Individuality, as One of the Elements of Well-Being."

ARGUMENTS FOR INDIVIDUALITY

Chapter three of *On Liberty*, like *The Subjection of Women*, begins with a pessimistic note about the unwillingness of the audience to give any credence to the claim that certain ends, like reforming the legal system or establishing a set of social arrangements which give free scope to individuality, are worth pursuing: "the greatest difficulty to be encountered [in arguing for extensive freedom of action] does not lie in the appreciation of means towards an acknowledged end, but in the indifference of persons in general to the end itself (18: 261)." Mill seeks to persuade readers that:

Acts, of whatever kind, which, without justifiable cause, do harm to

---

[1] See the notices in *The Saturday Review*, the *British Quarterly*, and *Bentley's Quarterly*, reprinted in *Liberty: Contemporary Responses to John Stuart Mill*, ed. Andrew Pyle, (Thoemmes Press: Bristol, 1994), pp. 6-24, 184-209, 210-54.

[2] Bell's essay is reprinted in *Liberty: Contemporary Responses to John Stuart Mill*, ed. Andrew Pyle, (Thoemmes Press: Bristol, 1994), pp. 118-58.

[3] See, for example, the essays by James MacKenzie, Herbert Cowell, and John Wilson, reprinted in *Liberty: Contemporary Responses to John Stuart Mill*, ed. Andrew Pyle, (Thoemmes Press: Bristol, 1994), pp. 386-408, 298-320, 321-48.

106   *John Stuart Mill's Deliberative Landscape*

> others, may be, and in the more important cases absolutely require to
> be, controlled by the unfavorable sentiments, and, when needful, by
> the active interference of mankind. The liberty of the individual must
> thus far be limited; he must not make himself a nuisance to other
> people. But if he refrains from molesting others in what concerns
> them, and merely acts according to his own inclination and judgment
> in things which concern himself, the same reasons which show that
> opinion should be free, prove also that he should be allowed, without
> molestation, to carry his opinions into practice at his own cost (18:
> 260).

The chapter devoted to this topic has attracted a lot of comment and criticism. I won't enter into the more familiar debates about the arguments.[5]
But *that* Mill argued for his maxim is all by itself interesting.

Here's why. Mill takes it that the sources of opposition to his view are
legion, and, by the end of this brief chapter, his account of the forces ranged
against individuality has gone considerably beyond "indifference to the
end." The English, of course, pride themselves on progressivism. But what
his audience has in view in advocating progressive social policies falls well
short of what Mill seeks:

> we are eager for improvement in politics, in education, even in
> morals, though in this last our idea of improvement chiefly consists
> in persuading or forcing other people to be as good as ourselves. It is
> not progress we object to; on the contrary, we flatter ourselves that we
> are the most progressive people who ever lived. It is individuality we
> war against: we should think we had done wonders if we made our-
> selves all alike; forgetting that unlikeness of one person to another is
> generally the first thing which draws the attention of either to the
> imperfection of his own type, and the superiority of another, or the
> possibilities of combining the advantages of both, of producing some-
> thing better than either (18: 273).

This "forgetfulness," and the war against the individual, leads increasingly
to a blunting of differences, and the great leveling is amply assisted by
larger forces of social change:

> The circumstances which surround different classes and individuals,
> and shape their characters, are daily becoming more assimilated.
> Formerly, different ranks, different neighbourhoods, different trades
> and professions, lived in what might be called different worlds; at
> present, to a great degree in the same. Comparatively speaking, they
> now read the same things, listen to the same things, see the same

---

[4] In *Liberty: Contemporary Responses to John Stuart Mill*, ed. Andrew Pyle, (Thoemmes
Press: Bristol, 1994), pp. 398-99.

Liberty, Ideals and Moral Nature   107

> things, go to the same places, have their hopes and fears directed to
> the same objects, have the same rights and liberties, and the same
> means of asserting them. Great as are the differences of position
> which remain, they are nothing to those which have ceased. And the
> assimilation is still proceeding. All the political changes of the age
> promote it, since they all tend to raise the low and to lower the high.
> Every extension of education promotes it, because education brings
> people under common influences, and gives them access to the gen-
> eral stock of facts and sentiments (18: 274-75).

The list of forces conducive to conformity continues: greater means of communication, increased commerce and trade, large-scale manufacture, etc.
He concludes this litany by remarking: "The combination of all these causes forms so great a mass of influences hostile to Individuality, that it is not
easy to see how it can stand its ground" (18: 275).

How does Mill respond to the challenge of persuading his audience to
side with liberty and individuality in the face of all this? He is asking his
audience to support and protect individuality, a thing which they not only
do not value, but are hostile toward. By associationist lights, his only hope
for success will lie in getting his audience to form an attachment of some
sort to individuality, to come to associate it with some potential source of
pleasure or pain-exemption, to move from a "con-attitude" to a "pro-attitude." But look what happens: in the face of their antipathy, in the face of
vast social change all tending toward the production of conformist mediocrity, Mill *argued*. He didn't edit an anthology of different sorts of poetry.
He didn't write a novel. He didn't sing a song. He didn't consult a chemist.
He argued. This is a very strange thing to do under the circumstances and
it points to an optimism about the power of intellect to sway feeling and
shape ends that has no easy place in Mill's official moral psychology.[6]

In this chapter, I will consider several ways in which an associationist
might be justified in resorting to argument to sway feeling. I will conclude
by suggesting that none of these makes sense of what Mill is up to in
Chapter Three of *On Liberty*.

COULD THE ARGUMENTS BE CALCULATIVE?

Now, it might be thought that argument wasn't in the least strange. For
example, if Mill was simply arguing that support for giving the freest possible rein to the variety of characters was itself a means to an acknowledged

---

[5] My path will take some of its direction from Isaiah Berlin's writings on Mill,
however. See *Four Essays on Liberty*, (Oxford University Press: Oxford, 1969), pp.
118-206.

John Stuart Mill's Deliberative Landscape

shared end, then his appeal to the intellects of his readers could be seen as turning on a completely straightforward bit of calculative practical reasoning. Calculative practical reasoning can take one of two forms: it can involve finding means to antecedently given ends, or it can involve articulating the parts of some larger whole end, such that the whole can then be attained by attaining the parts.

I already have touched upon the argument from ignorance—in seeking the greatest balance of pleasure over pain, one's best hope is to seek out a lifestyle suited to one's type and freedom of action gives people the elbow room they need in order to conduct experiments in living and find lives that suit them. It is a means-end argument. The end is achieving the greatest happiness for the greatest number of people. The means is allowing room for experiments in living. The argument does not work. And the seriousness of its failure as a bit of calculative reasoning seems even more glaring in light of Mill's subsequent account of all the forces which conspire to reduce the varieties in types of persons. Calculative arguments only work on people who *have* the ends served or attained by the means or parts put forth in the argument. The argument from ignorance operates by way of several assumptions, among them, that we want the greatest happiness for the greatest number among us no matter what types of people are to be found at large in the general populace. As Mill's criticism of English "progressiveness" suggests, he is addressing readers who do not have *that* end. His readers would rather press toward greater conformity, and then create a climate favorable to the satisfactions of uniformity. This, too, is a route to more happiness for more people. It is just a route that involves changing people so that more of them can find happiness in the status quo, rather than changing the status quo to accommodate more kinds of people.

There are other strands of means-end practical argument presented in the chapter. Mill prefaces these by insulting those of his readers who understand what individuality comes to, and nevertheless will require means-end

---

[6] The easiest way for him to cope with explaining *why* he argues when he argues would be to treat *On Liberty* as an exercise in eloquence—the attempt to sway an audience's feelings by effective use of rhetoric. Eloquence, recall, works on inferior minds as an external spur to feeling. In this case, then, Mill might be relying upon his understanding of his audience's feelings, together with a sense for which thoughts they will find compelling, in order to alter subtle features of complex states of mind. And here, the explanation for why Mill argues might be that his chief strengths are intellectual, that he could not hope to pen verse or novels that would sway the audience's feelings. Mill might have given some such account of his efforts if he had been pressed on the point. He might also have pointed out that he was adverting to ideals, ideational contents to which positive feelings "cling" ordi-

Liberty, Ideals and Moral Nature   *109*

reasons for supporting it:

> Having said that Individuality is the same thing with development, and that it is only the cultivation of individuality which produces, or can produce, well-developed human beings, I might here close the argument: for what more or better can be said of any condition of human affairs, than that it brings human beings themselves nearer to the best they can be? or what worse can be said of any obstruction to good, than that it prevents this? Doubtless, however, these considerations will not suffice to convince those who most need convincing; and it is necessary further to show, that these developed human beings are of some use to the undeveloped—to point out to those who do not desire liberty, and would not avail themselves of it, that they may be in some intelligible manner rewarded for allowing other people to make use of it without hindrance (18: 267).

The use of "rewarded" is telling in two ways. First, juvenile adults—those mediocre people susceptible to narrative art, recall—never break free of the genetic structure of their associative system. *Volitional* associative histories begin in early childhood moral education. What holds sway in an average sort of early moral education is "the old familiar instruments, praise and blame, reward and punishment" (1:141). How children and adults with undeveloped minds operate is as hedonic calculators. We are on familiar turf. Second, notice that Mill is indeed proceeding as if his task was *to alter his readers' proximate ends.* Those readers who do not take an interest in development will want to see what they stand to gain if they nevertheless support policies which conduce to individuality. For these readers, Mill then provides additional means-end considerations in support of promoting considerations favorable to individuality (that the developing individual might find an improved way of doing what the customary people seek also to do, for instance, or invent something that can be made use of more generally, or keep us on our toes and so keep us prepared to defend our own opinions and actions, conformist though they be).

---

narily. But I rather suspect that if positive feelings "cling" ordinarily to thought about vitality, honor, nobility, etc., this is *on account* of their content and moral force, rather than it being the case that such notions have moral force on account of the tendency of good feeling to "cling" to them. The soundness of an evaluative judgment about the place of autonomy and the like in a happy life, notice, does not depend upon the *kind of mind* to which it is addressed or from which it proceeds. And if we are persuaded about the place of these ideals in a flourishing human life, it ought to be because the arguments Mill makes are good, not because Mill has ingeniously anticipated the character of future audiences' feelings, and so used masterful eloquence to pull us along with him.

But the title of his chapter is "Individuality, as One of the Elements of Well-Being," suggesting that the principle argument at issue, if it is calculative, is of the part-whole, rather than means-end, variety. So, in assessing how far this argument is in keeping with the remaining instrumentalist structure of Mill's moral psychology, I will set out to assess whether or not the main argument can be read as a part-whole bit of calculative practical reasoning. I will call the argument that we ought to promote individuality because it is a part of well-being the "argument from ideals." In the means-end arguments, promoting individuality is offered as a means to securing the general welfare. In the argument from ideals Mill instead insists that, under conditions of modernity, individuality is part of well-being, hence, seeking a greater measure of well-being for a greater number of people requires (in part) promoting individuality.

Both the means-end and part-whole defenses of liberty of action are broadly consistent with the second position on pleasure that I sketched near the conclusion of the last chapter: the attachment of (a-rational, felt) pleasure to ideas and impressions is governed by many forces. In means-end arguments, stress is placed upon patterns of passive susceptibilities as determinants of happiness (Mill argues both that freedom of action permits people to use experiments in living to find the lives suitable to their "types," and that, no matter what one's type, one could stand to benefit from the fruits of others' experiments in living, in part because there may be sufficient overlap in types to make the results of different sorts of people's experiments broadly applicable, and in part because exposure to variety helps keep us on our toes and prompts us to defend our own typical modes of living). The argument from ideals, however, turns on the interconnections among ideals which direct individuals to make the best of themselves.

In the argument from ideals, sound evaluative judgment about the place of moral self-perfection, character development, individuality, vitality, and the like, in human life *generally* are evinced in offering a utilitarian defense of liberty. Happiness, according to the part-whole argument, consists in part in having a healthy appreciation of one's own best potential and striving to realize it in one's character and actions.

THE ARGUMENT FROM IDEALS AS A PART-WHOLE ARGUMENT

The part-whole argument from ideals goes by way of a series of apparently innocent equivalences, beginning from the premise that no sensible person holds that a good *human* life can be lived by a person who never develops

Liberty, Ideals and Moral Nature

"any of the qualities which are the distinctive endowment of a human being" (18: 262). The premise is innocuous enough. And here come the initial equivalence claims:

1. The qualities that are the distinctive endowment of a human being include the "human faculties of perception, judgment, discriminative feeling, mental activity, and...moral preference" (18: 262).
2. A faculty is a power, and hence can only develop when exercised.
3. The distinctively human faculties "are exercised only in making a choice" (18: 262).
4. The best exercise will then come in the most important choice, which is the choice of one's "plan of life": "He who chooses his plan for himself employs all his faculties. He must use observation to see, reasoning and judgment to foresee, activity to gather materials for decision, discrimination to decide, and when he has decided, firmness and self-control to hold to his deliberate decision" (18: 262-63); thus he who chooses his own life plan gets the exercise requisite to development.

But the exercise of intellect and will-power alone do not suffice to determine a man's course. The spirit of his undertaking comes from his "desires and impulses" (18: 263). And here there is some danger that Mill's readers will be glad to let a person go her own way *provided* that her desires and impulses are customary ones, that is, that her affective states are conventional. They will be much less likely to welcome independence in a person whose feelings and inclinations are deeply unconventional. Why? Because it is unconventional *feelings* (on this view) that lead people to do unconventional things, and what Mill's audience detests is independent, unconventional action. (Unconventional feelings, by the lights of Mill's associationism, will be pleasures associated with attainment of unconventional ends.) Moreover, the threat of the unanticipated, unconventional act will be felt by his audience as the threat of the unconscionable act. They associate strong, uncustomary feeling with bold, immoral action. And here comes the next claim:

5. "There is no natural connexion between strong impulses and a weak conscience. The natural connexion is the other way" (18: 263).

Mill supports his claim that the connection tends in this direction "naturally" through another series of equivalence claims:

6. If we say that "one person's desires and feelings are stronger and more various than those of another" we have merely said that the

first person "has more of the raw material of human nature" than the second (18: 263).

7. While having more than the average allotment of the raw material of human nature in one *may* make one capable of doing more harm than is the average person, it "certainly" makes one capable of doing "more good" than the average person (18: 263); that is, the surplus is not sufficient for production of an extraordinarily good person, but it is necessary.

8. Furthermore, "Strong impulses are but another name for energy," and "more good may always be made of an energetic nature, than of an indolent and impassive one" (18: 263).

9. And in this same vein: the very "same strong susceptibilities which make the personal impulses vivid and powerful, are also the source from whence are generated the most passionate love of virtue, and the sternest self-control" (18: 263-64).

Mill concludes that it is by fostering conditions which conduce to the "cultivation" of strong impulses, feelings, and desires, steered by means of a strong will and the distinctively human intellectual faculties "that society both does its duty and protects its interests: not by rejecting the stuff of which heroes are made because it knows not how to make them" (18: 264).

Society, he explains, could not set itself the task of *making* "heroes" even if it wanted to. There is *no other means* to the production of excellent human beings under conditions of modernity than leaving room for substantial independence of thought, discussion, and, above all, action because (and here comes the crowning equivalence):

10. "A person whose desires and impulses are his own—are the expression of his own nature, as it is developed and modified by his own culture—is said to have a character. One whose impulses and desires are not his own, has no character, no more than a steam-engine has a character...Whoever thinks that individuality of desires and impulses should not be encouraged to unfold itself, must maintain that society has no need of strong natures—is not the better for containing many persons of much character—and that a high general average of energy is not desirable" (18: 264).

The argument, that is, proceeds by linking up ideals of energy, self-determination, humanity, character, and development in such a way as to suggest that squeamishness about unconventional lifestyles is roughly equivalent to refusal of the conditions necessary for the development of character in an overall climate of social vitality. In this sense, the part-whole argument presents itself as a *reductio*.

How does the part-whole argument stand with respect to the means-

Liberty, Ideals and Moral Nature   *113*

end arguments? The two kinds of argument, if both are, indeed, calculative, should operate in tandem. Here's how: the principle of utility which sets the standard for the defense of liberty requires that Mill show that liberty conduces to overall well-being. The linkage between having a character and well-being will come by way of Mill's account of the higher pleasures as the fruits of developing harmonious, whole states of mind, organized by strong thought and cultivated feeling. So the suggestion that those who avail themselves of opportunities for self-culture will thereby enjoy more pleasant lives is secured by Mill's revisions to associationist doctrine. But those who are disinclined to make use of such liberties will not only fail to enjoy the higher fruits of self-culture, they will also be made uncomfortable by the presence of strong, passionate, smart, solid individuals in their world. In what sense, then, will liberty conduce to the well-being of the remaining (and numerically greater) portion of the citizens? By offering them rewards that they might not otherwise get.

I think that this is, actually, exactly how Mill means his argument to go. But I also think that the argument is plagued by all sorts of difficulties, if it is read in light of the implicit calculative picture of practical reason. I think this because Mill's claims about self-culture in *On Liberty* take us considerably beyond the revisions to associationist moral psychology that he made in the wake of his mental crisis. I will make my argument for this point in stages, beginning by linking up elements in the part-whole argument with elements in the revised moral psychology. This step sets up the explicit connection between happiness and individuality. Next I will argue that, for all the similarities between the *Liberty*'s stress on self-culture and the emphasis on mental cultivation in the writings on poetry and psychology, the stress on self-determination in the *Liberty* involves Mill in a subtle change of topics.

AUTOMATONS IN HUMAN FORM

Mill's part-whole argument centers on the importance of fashioning one's own will, of individuality, of self-culture. Elsewhere Mill writes:

> There is no need to expiate on the deficiencies of a system of ethics which does not pretend to aid individuals in the formation of their own character; which recognises no such wish as that of self-culture, we may even say no such power, as existing in human nature; and if it did recognise, could furnish little assistance...because it overlooks the existence of about half of the whole number of mental feelings which human beings are capable of, including all those of which the direct objects are states of their own mind (10: 98).

The posture of nonviolent introspection which comes through, e.g., poetic associations is one sort of mental feeling directed at one's own state of mind. The whole business of self-culture directs one to take up a posture of nonviolent (i.e., developmental rather than dissolving analytical) introspection as well. The free scope that is meant to be given to varieties of character is, that is, free scope for the development of a motivational sets rooted in harmonious, whole states of mind, or so I will argue. The textual evidence for the claim is ample, but some of it is most quickly assembled in light of Mill's metaphors. I will turn to these next by way of linking his revisions to associationism with his stress on self-culture.

Mill's early motivational set had been fashioned after the design of his father and Bentham. In light of the stress on self-determination in the *Liberty* it seems clear that this, all by itself, had been part of the younger Mill's problem. A man who has not undertaken to form his own will, whose desires and impulses are merely the products of his early education, circumstances and cultural setting, does not just have an "unconfirmed" or defective character, he has *no character at all*, "no more than a steam-engine has character" (18: 264).

Note the allusion to mechanism in the steam engine comparison. Mill uses the danger of mechanism to great effect in *On Liberty*. He warns, for instance, of the "tendency in the best beliefs and practices to degenerate into the mechanical" without "a succession of persons whose ever-recurring originality prevents the grounds of those beliefs and practices from becoming merely traditional" (18: 267). The best employment of the machine image comes in the passage where Mill makes most extensive use of it, the robot thought experiment:

> Supposing it were possible to get houses built, corn grown, battles fought, causes tried, and even churches erected and prayers said, by machinery—by automatons in human form—it would be a considerable loss to exchange for these automatons even the men and women who at present inhabit the more civilized parts of the world, who assuredly are but starved specimens of what nature can and will produce. Human nature is not a machine to be built after a model, and set to do exactly the work prescribed for it, but a tree, which requires to grow and develope [*sic*] itself on all sides, according to the tendency of the inward forces which make it a living thing (18: 263).

Throughout the essay, Mill sets up a contrast between vital human nature and "blind and simply mechanical" modes of thought, feeling, action.[7] The same contrast organized Mill's account of his mental crisis and his discussion of the difference between his father's psychological doctrines (based in

Liberty, Ideals and Moral Nature 115

mechanical laws of association) and the principles operative in mental chemistry. I will next turn to these.

Mill resorts to mechanical metaphors frequently in illustrating *both* the problem with customary characters *and* the problem with Benthamite moral psychology. I take it that this is partly because what Bentham and James Mill got *right* was the moral psychology of the reactive average person who has "undeveloped" introspective capacities, an "undeveloped" intellect, and weak feelings. These are the people whose motivational sets retain the structure of the contingent order of experience. They are, Mill warns, on the ascendancy in England.

The volitional psychological states of undeveloped minds retain their genetic components as integrant parts. In Mill's revision, this kind of motivating association was contrasted with the fused, harmonious whole states of mind that informed the actions and responses of cultivated people. Explaining the contrast, Mill wrote: "the laws of the phenomena of mind are sometimes analogous to mechanical, but sometimes also to chemical laws" (8: 853). His father's moral psychology was, in the relevant sense, mechanical. The associated components retain their character and function when they are combined with other ideational or affective bits. They are like cogs and wheels which hook up in regular ways and jointly produce decision, action, thought, judgment. In mental chemistry, however, ideational and affective bits combine in ways that alter the character of the inputs: the raw materials cease to exist in their original form in their product (the whole state of mind). The character of the inputs can be recovered associatively, as one can recall what went into the batter before the cake was baked. But the "ingredients" of a whole state of mind cease to be parts of the whole state of mind.

In Chapter IV, I argued that one way of making some sense of Mill's assertions about the comparative superiority of the higher pleasures was just this:

1. A man experiencing a higher pleasure is enjoying a kind of delight that flows from a whole state of mind.
2. If he is capable of retrospective introspective analysis, he can recover by memory the "ingredients" that are combined in his whole state of mind.
3. Some of these "ingredients" are themselves associative states of the kind explained by James Mill's psychology; these associations give rise to lower pleasures (separable pleasures pursued as

---

[7] The quoted phrase is taken from Mill's discussion of the difference between thoughtful and uncritical adherence to custom (18: 263).

116 *John Stuart Mill's Deliberative Landscape*

> proximate ends of action—the stuff of hedonic calculation). This *must* be so, actually, because we can easily establish as a matter of fact that all associative systems crucially involve learning and every human being begins life as a little hedonic calculator.
> 4. Anyone experiencing higher pleasures who can recover the associative "ingredients" that serve as inputs to the chemically fused whole state is in a position to judge whether the higher pleasure of the whole state is preferable to the lower pleasures of the "ingredient" state.[8]

I thereby tried to link John Stuart Mill's otherwise perplexing remarks about the powers of those equipped to judge which pleasures are best to his theory of mental chemistry. Higher pleasures are grounded in harmonious, whole states of mind. We can tell an associationist story about where whole states of mind come from that equips those whose motivational systems are relevantly whole to judge the pleasures of another sort in comparison with their own even though these judges do not now experience those pleasures. It's a bit like judging that tasting a well-made cake is better than tasting the mixed dry ingredients, the mixed wet ingredients, the batter got by combining these, etc. To the extent that this sort of analogy works (and it is doubtful how workable the analogy is, of course), Mill has some grounds for his claims about those competent to pass judgment on pleasures.

The exclusive concern with mental mechanism allowed James Mill to give adequate treatment of intellectual and affective training, but prevented him from giving adequate attention to genuine intellectual and emotional cultivation. *Trained* feelings are precisely those that have been shaped by the familiar instruments of praise and blame, reward and punishment, and so made to fit the requirements of those who have taken charge of training. The merely trained intellect is likewise lacking in proper development. James Mill had given John Stuart intellectual training, but had failed to encourage him in self-culture. The result had been another form of mechanism. Mill was left with great capacities for set intellectual exercises of various sorts, but without any way of setting this skill in the context of a whole and balanced, harmonious psychological life. In his time of mental crisis, when he felt himself to have no reason to do much of anything, he still had been able to rely upon the "mechanical" activity of his intellect:

> During this time I was not incapable of my usual occupations. I went on with them mechanically, by the mere force of habit. I had been so drilled in a certain sort of mental exercise, that I could still carry on with it when all the spirit had gone out of it (1:143).

Liberty, Ideals and Moral Nature

Again, recollecting the period of his life just prior to his mental crisis he wrote, "I conceive that the description so often given of a Benthamite, as a mere reasoning machine...was during two or three years of my life not altogether untrue of me" (1: 111). The internal workings of the mere reasoning machine were, he explains, entirely given over the external stimuli, even when his feelings appeared to cling to higher ideas:

> Ambition and desire of distinction; I had in abundance; and zeal for what I thought the good of mankind was my strongest sentiment, mixing with and colouring all the others. But my zeal was as yet little else, at that period of my life, than zeal for speculative opinions. It had not its root in genuine benevolence, or sympathy with mankind; though these qualities held their due place in my ethical standard. Nor was it connected with any high enthusiasm for ideal nobleness (1: 113).

What his father had done (although the son shrank from saying so outright), was precisely to undertake the project of educating his son as though "human nature" was "a machine to be built after a model, and set to do exactly the work prescribed for it."

John Stuart Mill's rhetorical conduct, that is, is telling. The *Liberty's* contrast between customary people and those who cultivate individuality lines up with the contrast between mental mechanism and mental chemistry, the contrast between externally-directed motivation and introspectively cultivated, harmonious, whole states of mind, and the contrast between mediocrity and self-perfection. And this, in turn, signals that Mill's revisions to associationist moral psychology are crucial to understanding what he is advocating in *On Liberty*. And this looks to give the argument from ideals a kind of grounding in Mill's moral psychology.

Here's how. In *Utilitarianism* we learn that the best pleasures are the higher pleasures. If these are indeed the pleasures of cultivated, harmonious mental life, then they are the pleasures that come from intellectual, affective and practical cultivation. The quality of the higher pleasures is such that some higher pleasure outweighs a quantitatively greater measure of lower pleasure. To say that self-development is an element of well-being is

---

[8] In urging this, I quoted Mill: "the test of quality [of pleasure], and the rule for measuring it against quantity, being the preference felt by those who, in their opportunities of experience, to which must be added their habits of self-consciousness and self-observation, are best furnished with means of comparison" (10: 214). The "habits of self-consciousness and self-observation" must be added because, I think, these are the capacities which give them access by introspective analysis to the genetic parts of the whole state of mind.

to say that capacity for higher pleasures is an element of well-being. And the whole bulk of Mill's writings on taxonomic psychology and mental chemistry can then be brought forward to support the equivalence claims in the argument from ideals, for even though none of us could know what it would be like to live in a modern society as open and liberal as the one Mill describes, we can rely upon mind science to give us some grounds for thinking that it would make it more probable that persons in such a society might develop capacities for higher pleasures.

There is, however, a problem with this way of reading the argument. The problem is that the emphasis on self-determination in the *Liberty* takes us well past the point we reached in following Mill through his crisis, beyond even, what we can get by drawing heavily upon Mill's discussion of self-development in the *Logic*. I will take up these matters in the next two sections.

IMITATION VERSUS CULTIVATION

In his account of how art helped him, recall, Mill stressed the way in which reading poetry prompted him to a kind of half-unconscious mimicry. Poetry was an instrument of self-culture, recall, because poems sometimes presented superior states of mind, and in the simple act of comprehending a well-fashioned poem, a reader found herself forming a state of mind just like the poet's by drawing on the raw materials provided by her own habitual associations and allowing these to rearrange themselves on the model of the poem's imagery. Poets instructed by example. Readers learned by taking up the perspective of the poet. The quality of the teaching provided in verse depended upon the moral qualities of the whole state of mind expressed in the poem. But if the poet was both good at his craft, possessed of lofty thoughts, and capable of evoking finer feelings in verse, one could get a better character by reading. Indeed, this was crucial to Mill's account of how reading poetry resulted in his own character development.

Notice: the fact that the instrument of culture in this story was *Wordsworth's* state of mind makes *no* difference to Mill's insistence that he, John Mill, emerged from reading Wordsworth with a finer character than he, John Mill, had before he took up reading Wordsworth. There seemed to be no question, even, that Mill's moral improvement resulted from taking up *Wordsworth's* perspective on life. The result was not a new mode of expression for Mill's own impulses. The result was a *change* in Mill's impulses.

There is, of course, a trivial sense in which the "desires and impulses"

Liberty, Ideals and Moral Nature

ignited by reading poetry were Mill's "own": his intact passive susceptibility to rural imagery, and his sympathy for Wordsworth's thoughts were both involved in making it possible for Mill to use Wordsworth as an instrument of self-culture. Then too, Mill's own dissatisfaction with his old character had been the spur to change, so he had had a wish of his own for something better than what he could make of himself. This was, of course, very necessary. Only when a man has such a wish, he can begin to take charge of the reformation of his character:

> Our character is formed by us as well as for us; but the wish which induces us to attempt to form it is formed for us; and how? Not, in general, by our organization, nor wholly by our education, but by our experience; experience of the painful consequences of the character we previously had: or by some strong feeling of admiration or aspiration, accidentally aroused...And indeed, if we examine closely, we shall find that this feeling, of our being able to modify our own character *if we wish*, is itself the feeling of moral freedom which we are conscious of. A person feels morally free who feels that his habits or his temptations are not his masters, but he theirs: who even in yielding to them knows that he could resist; that were he desirous of altogether throwing them off, there would not be required for that purpose a stronger desire than he knows himself to be capable of feeling (8: 840-41).

You have to have it in you to want something different for yourself in order to undertake a process of self-culture. The desire for character-change was Mill's own. The choice of poets to read in effecting magically fused, harmonious and whole states of mind was Mill's own. The raw materials that provided the genetic parts by which the poetry could work its magic were also Mill's own. But "own" here just means something like "rightly ascribed to M," and in *that* sense of "own," the resulting whole state of mind Mill produced in apprehending Wordsworth's poetry was *not*, strictly, Mill's own. It was *Wordsworth's*. Mill was just following Wordsworth's lead.

Nowhere in the account of the special power of poetic association does Mill show any squeamishness about his imitation of Wordsworth. *Nowhere* is there anything like the contempt expressed in *On Liberty* for "the ape-like [faculty] of imitation" (18: 262). That is, even though it looks as though the part-whole argument in the *Liberty* is not only covering some of the same ground we found in Mill's writings on art, whole states of mind, and higher pleasures, and even though Mill employs some of the same rhetorical moves in both this essay and the other's I've touched upon—the same mechanical metaphors, the same allusions to nature, harmony and vitality, etc.,—something is very different this time around.

In *On Liberty*, Mill stresses individual efforts at self-perfection conducted under the guidance of very general ideals. The stress is upon a kind of self-determination, rather than upon unselfconsciously copying the better mindsets of better men. And the activity involved in developing such a base of practical operations, individuality, is no longer figured as primarily a species of morally ambitious mimicry.

It could be thought that Mill's own change of heart was an instance of a merely mechanical person (young John Stuart Mill) learning a better way of living from a proper individual (Wordsworth). This is, after all, how Mill describes what happened. But if their exchange is understood in those terms, then it isn't, strictly, necessary that a man choose his own plan of life in order to develop himself on all sides, much less that there be an overall climate conducive to self-development surrounding people who would do so. Wordsworth may have gone his own way in the world. Mill went the way that his father had directed him to go. Neither had the benefit of a society conducive to free full self-development. It is abundantly clear that the force of custom and convention was very costly to Mill, of course. It is abundantly clear that having another man choose a direction for Mill's own life was a great stress upon him as well. But that is not how the argument from ideals goes.

The argument from ideals doesn't turn on a cost-benefit analysis. It turns on claiming that *saying p* is the same thing as *saying q*. Cost-benefit analyses require some sort of empirical evidence for their support. Mill insists that no one has enjoyed the kinds of conditions of life he argues that we all ought to promote. So there is no experiential evidence to point to in running a cost-benefit argument. The question then becomes how his work in psychology might license the claims he makes on behalf of individuality. And this is the direction we would *have* to go in seeking the grounds for the argument, partly because, rather than consistently appealing to the special sensitivities and special needs of different kinds of people (individuated on the basis of their systems of passive susceptibilities), Mill instead has moved into a discussion of human nature more generally. The *general* account of human nature concerns "the qualities which are the distinctive endowment of a human being" (18: 262). Support for the general claims could be drawn from work on human psychology generally. Mill has a lot of such work to draw upon. The question becomes whether *that* work can be brought to bear on the task of supporting *these* claims.

The distinctive endowment of our kind lay in our power to shape our own characters and grow, and develop in light of ideals. I want now to sug-

Liberty, Ideals and Moral Nature 121

gest that what we see in Mill's part-whole argument is an altered picture of character, and that the change in that picture signals a change in topics on Mill's part. This change in topics, I will urge, marks a break between individuality and Mill's work on character-change and character-development.

Two Senses of "Character"

Character figured prominently in Mill's writings on art and his mental crisis. It also figures prominently in his writings on individuality. Character, in all of these, is intimately connected with "habits of willing," or "purposes" (8: 842). And in all of these writings, character is a thing that adults have and infants do not. But the kind of character at issue in the *Liberty*'s part-whole argument is different from the kind of character at issue in the taxonomic writings. And this suggests that the part-whole, ideal-based argument and the means-end, taxonomy-based argument come apart. Or so I will argue.

In the account of individuality, it is a necessary condition on having cultivated one's individuality that one be acting from what Mill calls a "confirmed character" in his book on logic (8: 843). To have a confirmed character is to have "a completely fashioned will" (8: 843). Mill wrote:

It is only when our purposes have become independent of the feelings of pain or pleasure from which they originally took their rise that we are said to have a confirmed character (8: 842-43).

So far, all that this does is to establish a distinction between mediocre minds and cultivated minds. Mediocre minds retain the shape of their associative histories. Mental chemistry alters the character of the cultivated mind in such a way that purposes "become independent of the feelings of pain or pleasure from which they originally took their rise." So far, there's no hint that a character borrowed from the poetry shelves of the lending library will be defective. After all, we know from the story of Mill's recovery that it is possible to induce cultivated mental states in oneself by reading poetry, that the copied states of mind are "chemically" fused rather than "mechanically" soluble into their genetic parts, etc., and in this sense, that whole states of mind got by imitation are relevantly "independent" of their source materials. Such states might be reinforced and permanently enshrined at the core of one's character by habitual adventures in reading. Reading very well-crafted and good poetry is, in this sense, an instrument of self-culture, since one cannot understand such verse without forming compelling, indissoluble motivating associations.

In his taxonomic writings, the compelling force of an association gave evidence that it was well-suited to one's nature or temperament. The man who stumbled onto his "natural" associations, if he was healthy and sane, ought precisely to have felt satisfied with his life. Indeed, the forcefulness of the motivating associations was what made of them a solid, extra-rational foundation for action. It was hard to see why it mattered that a man be left to his own devices in searching for the constituents of his happiness. It was hard to see why social engineering shouldn't have been employed in systematically forming men's characters. What mattered was the fitness of one's ends to one's passive susceptibilities, and it shouldn't have made a difference whether one discovered fitting pursuits by trial-and-error and experiments in living, or was simply relieved of the burden of doing so by a creditable, authoritative source of passive-susceptibility-profiling. For example, nothing in the account of how Wordsworth came to Mill's rescue turned on the fact that Mill had found Wordsworth all on his own. There was no hint that, had his father handed him the *Lyrical Ballads* and insisted that he have a look at them in order to get over his depression, the reading would somehow have been less beneficial. And if Mill was right about why Wordsworth could provide the very culture of feelings needed, it is hard to see why it mattered that Mill do more than be open to the poet's good influence. The *activity* involved in the whole state of mind Mill experienced reading Wordsworth was, by hypothesis, the result of copying the complex, associative activity in Wordsworth's mental state.

The account of confirmed character in the *Logic* leaves room for the possibility that adopting a plan of selective mimicry might be enough to produce a confirmed character. While Mill goes on to insist in the *Logic* that not just *anyone* can do the job of fashioning a will, that, in particular, if *other* people had done most of the work of fashioning a man's motivational set, then, no matter how beautifully they'd done their job, he did not have a confirmed character (8: 840), his discussion of taking charge of the business of one's own character formation is very nearly autobiographical, and there is no hint that pursuing an assigned reading program would not count as taking charge of character development. The urge to take charge of character-development, Mill explains, is prompted:

> Not, in general, by our organization, nor wholly by our education, but by our own experience; experience of the painful consequences of the character we previously had: or by some strong feeling of admiration or aspiration, accidentally aroused (8: 840-41).

Mill's program of self-culture had both sources: there was the pain of his old character and there was the accidental encounter with the admirable Wordsworth's superior mindset. Before finding Wordsworth, Mill *was* "the

Liberty, Ideals and Moral Nature

person [who felt] discouraged or paralysed by thinking himself unable" to change his character (8: 841; 1: 143). And how Mill undertook to change his character through reading was very much in line with the *Logic* account of this process. The account in the *Logic* stresses liberation from one's associative history, and devotes a special section to motives which do not rest in "anticipation of a pleasure or pain" (8: 842-43). Contrast this with the picture of self-culture that emerges from the series of equivalence claims in *On Liberty*.

The purposes of cultivated individual, for example, seem not to find their source in any kind of half-unconscious copying. Although character (in both the new and old senses) develops as "purposes" do (8: 842-43), the purposes of genuine individuals are not mere effects of bringing one's desires in line with some underlying pattern which can fuse one's feelings with one's thoughts. Instead, the purposes of someone who is cultivating proper individuality are the result of a taking charge of her will in a special way, a way that seems to require more than finding good role models.

In the *Liberty*, Mill continues to maintain that intellect alone can't induce a particular man to change his character—he had to want to improve himself before he could do so. But the human being, as such, aims to "perfect" itself, and the perfection of the self yields not just exceptionally fine exemplars of good sorts of people (which seemed to be what exposure to very good literature yielded), but rather originality and uniqueness. The exercise of liberty that Mill describes shows itself *not* in developing the a capacity to delight in a life plan set in place for one by, say, one's father (which is what Mill got by cultivating his feelings), but rather in independent choice of life-plans. And so on. In short, it looks very much as though Mill has taken all of his work on self-culture, work which stressed one's underlying passive susceptibilities, one's engagement with the people and activities and things of ordinary life, one's attachment to places and people, etc., and simply pushed it in the direction of a very strong emphasis on self-determination. But that push isn't warranted by the experience that went in to altering Mill's view of the human mind. That push looks instead to be a shift in topics.

Here's why. In the taxonomic writings, to have a character was simply to have a certain type of mind. In the argument from ideals, to have a character is to have been actively engaged in "fashioning" one's own will. In the taxonomic writings, "character" signified "only a certain state of feeling grown habitual" (1: 352). In the argument from ideals, "character" signifies the condition of a will that has been regulated in such a way that it is no longer swayed by habitual states of feeling. In the taxonomic writings, one could live one's life in accordance with one's father's design (as did John Stuart Mill) and still have a confirmed character (as is suggested by the autobiographical ring to the *Logic* account of confirmed character). In the argument from ideals, a man who has not chosen his own plan of life, and whose desires and impulses are not his own, does not just have an "unconfirmed" or defective character, he has *no character at all*, "no more than a steam-engine has character" (18: 264).

In short, what Mill is reaching for in the discussion of individuality as an element of well-being is more than he has grasped on in the other writings we've been looking at. And this, I will argue, makes reading the argument from ideals as a kind of calculative argument well nigh unsustainable. By involving a further change in the moral psychology it involves an as yet unforeseen shift in the account of happiness, one which would no longer appear to be grounded in the interestingly straightforward account of higher pleasures as rooted in whole states of mind. By reaching *striking* conclusions from a series of claims that seem to be intended as identity statements of some sort, it loses credibility as a part-whole calculative argument. By Mill's insistence that what he proposes has never been tried in a society like the one he's addressing, he seems to undercut any attempt to read the claims as empirical generalizations. And so on. I will run through these difficulties in the next section.

THE ARGUMENT FROM IDEALS

The move in the *Liberty* from the picture of character we have so far encountered to the powerful stress on originality and individuality comes in the shift from the claims about intellect, judgment and will-power to the claims about desires and impulses. Mill took it that his audience was happy to welcome individuality of discernment and substantial freedom of choice and action for people with conventional, customary desires and impulses. What worried them was allowing extensive freedom of action to people with unconventional feelings, desires, impulses, tastes. How Mill tried to convince them that this fear was unfounded was by making three points.

The third involved the assertion that powerful, unconventional feeling was more likely to prompt a strong conscience and passionate love of virtue than it was to prompt wildness and license. This is, of course, an empirical claim which would require empirical study for its support. Mill does little to support it. His second point was that "Strong impulses are but another name for energy," and "more good may always be made of an energetic nature, than of an indolent and impassive one" (18: 263). The difficulty

Liberty, Ideals and Moral Nature 125

with this claim rests in the modal. While it may be somehow true that "more good may always be made" of more "energy," he is asking his audience to *leave it to the energetic person* to determine *what* to make of her "surplus" energy. That she *could* become an extraordinarily valuable member of society is no reason to suppose that she *will*, at least not on the face of it. The slightly more interesting suggestion is the first, that if we say that "one person's desires and feelings are stronger and more various than those of another" we have merely said that the first person "has more of the raw material of human nature" than the second (18: 263). This claim lines up with the claim that individuality is nothing but development more clearly than do the other two: development is development of or in something on the order of "the raw material of human nature." But, again, it is hard to see how the mere fact that someone has a lot of raw material is a reason to suppose that she will produce a lot with it.

Now, all three claims are in the service of arguing that promoting individuality is necessary for promoting the greatest happiness for the greatest number, not that it is sufficient for it. Attaining a part of some whole end is necessary, but no sufficient, for attaining the whole. But the necessity claim is itself in jeopardy in this argument because of the emphasis on strong self-determination. Neither the reading of higher pleasures that I have been urging, nor the reading of character-development that came of following Mill through his mental crisis into literary theory and psychology licensed the suggestion that self-determination in a very strong sense was essential to self-development. Mill's burst into the territory of strong individuality did not come until very late in his life, when he took the floor in Parliament and threw his weight most strongly behind measures which lacked both popular support and legislative practicability. It is true that the section of his *Autobiography* devoted to his term in Parliament is longer than any chronologically comparable section of the book (those three years get more pages than the three years of his experience of and recovery from the first mental crisis, more pages than any other three years of his life). It is also true that he seems more pleased by what he did in Parliament than he was by any other thing that he did. But the stress on originality, uniqueness and the strong individual at the heart of the *Liberty*'s argument from ideals represents a break with the meticulous (however odd) attention to character-types and types of mental state that we found in his other writings on literature and psychology. It seems to have very little connection with most of Mill's work, actually, save a very early essay on genius, and the very late account of Mill's career in Parliament. The jargon of authenticity in the *Liberty* is out of step with the story of the human mind that Mill tells. I will turn now to explicit discussion of how this affects an attempt to read the argument from ideals as a bit of calculative practical reasoning.

All three of the claims about strong desires and strong impulses seem as though they might include claims about the likely outcome of leaving free scope for individuality. That is, it looks as though there might be a means-end side to the "part-whole" argument. They *shouldn't* be predictive claims, however. Claims about the likely outcome of allowing people substantial liberty of action are in some sense empirical. There is, however, nothing in *On Liberty* to suggest that Mill thinks that there is any historical basis at all for assessing the impact of a climate of freedom on the development of splendid individuals in a modern society. There has never been such an arrangement in such a society. Nor should it be the case that Mill is plotting a trajectory of development based on his observations of his fellows. His fellows are, for the most part, unlikely to become splendid individuals. They are instead precisely the people with conventional affections least likely to bother *anyone* if left to their own devices. Or so he seems to suggest, over and over again. Indeed, if he was making an empirical, calculative argument, he might do better to point out that it is extremely unlikely that anyone will make use of extensive liberty to do anything especially unconventional, and hence, harmless to support freedom of action, in roughly the way that despotic regimes can find it harmless to allow substantial freedom of the press if almost the whole of the oppressed population is illiterate. Print media gives the educated critics a place to complain, but fails to function as an instrument for the organization of resistance or uprising. Substantial freedom of action in a world where most people have weak feelings and mediocre intellects should likewise be fairly harmless. By the time their children are grown to maturity and are in a position to make use of the freedoms available, it is likely enough that no very great changes will happen. If anything, such rebellious inclinations as the next generation might harbor will have no very clear target, since the force of custom will be less burdensome for the few who would otherwise become strong rebels.

It might be thought that the outcome claims, if not grounded in actual experience, might somehow be consequences of the revisions Mill has made to associationist psychology (new expectations generated through the discovery of the new psychological processes which were chemical rather than mechanical). But here too we hit a wall. The *Liberty*'s stress on self-determination takes the chapter on individuality well beyond anything we encountered in Mill's writings on art, on his mental crisis, or even on character development in his *Logic*.

Liberty, Ideals and Moral Nature 127

Although Mill writes as though we should expect very good consequences of extensive liberties, the equivalence claims shouldn't be about likely outcomes. But not all part-whole arguments are about likely outcomes either, except in the sense that a good part-whole argument convinces people that doing what conduces to attaining *these* parts will *amount* to doing what conduces to attaining *this* whole. In this sense, a part-whole argument provides a practicable specification of a complex whole end. The problem with reading Mill's argument this way is just this: the whole end is self-perfection or self-beautification, and these, like the end of changing *something* about one's character in order to improve one's situation (Mill's "end" at the time of his crisis), are too indeterminate to support calculative part-whole reasoning.

Calculative part-whole reasoning is involved in things like wanting to make a chocolate cake and finding a good and practicable recipe. The relation between individuality, "energy," beauty, nobility, and perfection is not like that. This is why the crowning equivalence is not merely an "informative" identity statement, but a deeply *surprising* one. Who would have dreamed that "Whoever thinks that individuality of desires and impulses should not be encouraged to unfold itself, must maintain that society has no need of strong natures—is not the better for containing many persons of much character—and that a high general average of energy is not desirable" (18: 264)?! Who would have thought that having qualms about unconventional people leading unconventional lives where, say, one's children were likely to see it happening, was the same as wanting to deny that strong character was a good? Or that commitment to customary modes of marriage and family life meant commitment to an enervated society where belief had become a matter of mechanical adherence to dead dogma rather than a matter of seeking to hold living truth, where minds were bowed to yokes, where one ran the risk of having no character at all?

In short, the equivalence claims are too startling to count as a recognizable part-whole argument, and too untried to count as sound claims about the likely outcome of allowing free scope for a variety of characters. And these together, I take it, undermine the attempt to read Mill's decision to argue for his audience as a decision to provide a calculative account of why they should form a "pro-attitude" toward extensive freedom of action. We have, as near as I can tell, reached the end of the ways we might find of making sense of the argument from ideals on the basis of Mill's moral psychology, on the basis of Mill's commitment to empirical methods, on the basis of Mill's understanding of happiness, or on the basis of the apparent calculative structure of the chapter. By failing to find a way to

128   *John Stuart Mill's Deliberative Landscape*

assimilate this argument to some sort of calculative practical reasoning we
have, in turn I take it, failed to assimilate it to the account of pleasure that
is in keeping with such instrumentalism as remains in Mill's associationism.

THE BIFURCATED MIND IN THE ARGUMENT FROM IDEALS

The difficulty in finding adequate means of support for the claims that Mill
makes about why we ought to welcome strong unconventional characters
has its roots, I think, in his asking the reader to go from welcoming cultivated intellect and will-power in the service of *conventional* feelings to welcoming cultivated intellect and will-power in the service of *unconventional*
feelings. Desires and impulses (matters, at least in part, of feeling) were
treated as "raw materials" for action and character-development. What was
alarming to Mill's audience was in part, I suggest, the "rawness" of the
materials. Mill set up a picture in which it was possible to have a developed
and cultivated intellect *no matter what sort of feelings one had.* You could have
timid, customary, weak feelings and a cultivated intellect, or you could
have strong, unconventional, bold feelings and a cultivated intellect. Mill
seems willing to entertain the possibility that you could have seething,
rationally impenetrable passions of the kind one imagines Victorian imag-
inations conjured liberally, and a cultivated, well-developed intellect. The
terms in which he makes his argument, that is, presuppose the instrumentalist bifurcation of thought and feeling.

Drop this aspect of associationism, drop the skeletal remains of instrumentalism about reason in practice, and not only do these suggestions look
extremely dubious, but it becomes possible to run suitably amended versions the equivalence claims more successfully. What Mill wants is to set
up a strong rapport between virtue, reason, and powerful emotion. To the
extent that virtue is understood as a kind of corrective to temptation
(which is one traditional understanding of virtue, at least), it will be fairly
easy to argue that enervated, dull people will not be especially virtuous.
They will have no need of strong virtue. You need very little in the way of
courage, for example, if you are insensitive to danger, or if nothing you
would find yourself seeking to do requires much courage. If either your
imagination is weak or your inclinations are customary, it would be odd to
find you needing courage to carry on with your business. Similarly for other
virtues of the will, like prudence, patience and moderation. Similarly, if
you are a gentle person eager to please, you need very little of charity or
benevolence in you to keep you in harmony with your fellows. Rather, it is

Liberty, Ideals and Moral Nature 129

when you are prone to want things that are very much out of step with what those around you seek, or when you are highly imaginative or alive to many possibilities in your world that you have need of these sorts of virtues to get on well with your fellows, and need of the virtues of the will to get on well with your own affairs. This much seems entirely in keeping with Mill's claims about the raw materials of human nature and the strong attachment to virtue.

But suppose that Mill went for something stronger and (I think) less intuitive. Suppose Mill argued that genuine intellectual development was not possible without strong affections, not merely because the "juice" of thinking was feeling, but also because the strength of feeling came in part from its content. Suppose that he were to deny the implicit suggestion that a person of few and moderate passions can for all that have a well-developed intellect. He seemed to be moving in that direction in urging that the intellect is "stunted" without an appreciation for Beauty. Aesthetic sensitivity was treated by Mill, recall, as largely a matter of having peculiar capacities for pleasure. So there was a suggestion that without some kinds of strong affective capacities there could not be a cultivated (rather than merely trained) intellect. But suppose that rather than falling in with the (still) common assumption that emotion undoes reason, one took the position that uninspired, disinterested, passion-less reason was at best trained, that it betokened not a strong intellect, but some undetached trained intellect-parts?

Mill, I think, is sometimes on the verge of taking just this tack. It is a tack that would help his argument in the *Liberty* considerably. What gets him into trouble in that argument is sliding into the supposition that we could find a person of powerful and "authentically" owned desires and impulses who might fail to steer a reasonable course in her unconventional life, while allowing that we could find plenty of people with weak and undeveloped feelings laid out along customary lines who could enjoy cultivated intellects and virtue and would *not* feel it a great imposition to allow the force of custom to remain as it was. The question was, why not just let the force of social change and custom continue on its course, moving toward a new orthodoxy, and reduce the likelihood that people with strong unconventional desires and impulses will crop up in our midst and make life less comfortable? Why not let individuals get lost in the crowd?

The answer that Mill gives doesn't seem to work in these terms. It would work better if he instead claimed that part of what marks out desires and impulses as one's own is that they take unconventional objects, unconventional turns, seek out unconventional modes of expression in action, etc.

130   *John Stuart Mill's Deliberative Landscape*

and do so *because* they bear the imprint of unconventionally strong intellectual powers, that what we see in conventional people isn't good intellect and weak feeling, but rather deficient intellectual development and deficient feeling. If this were the case, then you really *couldn't* stifle individuality and expect developed people. The thought that you could would rest upon a mistake about the sensitivity of intellect to affect, and affect to intellect, and the way in which it is strength in both of these interconnected regions that requires moral strength to balance and direct it. This is, I think, the sort of thing that Mill both needs and can't bring himself to go for.

In the *Liberty*, Mill discusses the activity of *the* human being, rather than the fortunes of different kinds of men and women as subject to their natures and circumstance. "The" human being is not an average human being. Nor is it just any unusual human being. The human being is a creature capable of taking charge of the formation of its own character. The human being, further, needs to give attention to the formation of its character, because the human being has a jointly strong intellectual and affective nature, and it is a task of virtue to balance and coordinate strengths for the sake of sound action. In the process of developing itself, the human being is charged with exercising and developing its faculties in making choices, and the significance of the faculties lies in the contribution they make to action (they set *the* human being apart from *the* ape, for instance). The aim of the characteristic human activity is to express, "perfect," and "beautify" human nature. We expect that any particular woman or man will falter when "exercising" the distinctively human powers, but that is beside the point. The point is that she or he *must* exercise them in order to be more than a weak and "starved specimen." Indeed, freedom to engage in the exercise is more important than any result obtained thereby. All of the *results* could be achieved by automatons in human form (and if we had a divine calculator, then all of the means-ends reasoning could be performed by machine as well). If the human being is "naturally" aimed at making the best of itself that it can, if the human is a strong specimen in virtue of both its intellectual and its affective capacities, if the two can't, in practice or principle, be treated as separable, then the fact that a given human being has a lot of the raw material of human nature in her may give us the thought that she ought to be working toward making more of herself than someone with less of the stuff of humanity could. It is part of her humanity to try, and whatever in her would lead her to take *either* the stuff of her desires and impulses, *or* the stuff of her intellect, in another direction is a perversion of her (moral) nature rather than an expression of it. In short, if

Liberty, Ideals and Moral Nature 131

Mill were to build a tendency to seek what is best and most worthy into his understanding of human nature, and were he to refuse the separation of affect and intellect that he retains from his father's work in psychology, then the equivalence claims might begin to work. *Without* doing these things, however, it is hard to see how this argument is going to go.

To run the kind of argument I am imagining for Mill, of course, one would have to refuse the treatment of feeling (pleasure and pain) as primitive and juice-like. One would have to refuse much of the associationist picture of the mind. And one would have to rid oneself of the vestigial instrumentalism that continued to haunt Mill's moral psychology.

Index

Anderson, Elizabeth, *49*
Anscombe, G. E. M., 20-21
associationism. *See* de Cardaillac, Jean Jacques Séverin; instrumentalism about practical reason, relation to associationist psychology; Mill, James, psychology; Mill, John Stuart, on associationist accounts of mental phenomena; mind, laws governing association of ideas and impressions
Audi, Robert, 23
Austin, Charles, *3*, 8
Austin, John, *3*, 4
Burns, J. H., *13*
Bain, Alexander, 8, 27, *42*, *92*, *93*, 94
Bell, Robert, 104
Bentham, Jeremy:
    and consequentialism, 33, 35, 37-38, 39, 67-68, 76, 103
    and instrumentalism about practical reason, 17-18, 27-29, 33-38, 39, 43-44, 61, 62, 74, 76
    character of, 68
    on hedonic calculation, 29, 33, 35-39, 44, 46, 48, 61, 62, 64, 67-68, 74, 76, 82-83, 91, 96
    on hedonism, 33, 35-36, 45-46, 74-75, 82-84, 103
    on legislation, 33-35
    on morals, 33, 36-38
Berlin, Isaiah, 2, 9, 10, 35, *106*
Bersani, Leo, *31*
Carlisle, Janice, *6*, 7
Cowell, Herbert, *11*, *104*
Crisp, Roger, *81*
egoism, 25-26, 33
Dawson, Carl, *13*
de Cardaillac, Jean Jacques Séverin, 70-71, 75-76
Dewey, John, 18-19, 22
Fox, William, 4
Gauthier, David, 24, 30
Graham, George, *3*
Hardy, Harriet. *See* Harriet Taylor
Harris, Abram, *13*
happiness, 28-29, 33-34, 35-36, 37-38, 39, 41, 43, 44, 46, 47-48, 56, 59, 60, 74, 81-83, 84, 91, 92-94, 98-100, 101,

133

103, 108, 110, 113, 117, 122, 125, 127
Hempel, Carl, *19-20*
higher pleasures. *See* Mill, John Stuart, on higher and lower pleasures
Hobbes, Thomas, 22, 25-26, 27, 30, 33
Hume, David, 22, 25-26, 30, *33*, 94
Hyde, Thomas, *3*
instrumentalism about practical reason:
    and the arbitrariness problem, 35-36, 39, 43-46, 47, 49-50, 91-92, 101.
    and bifurcated accounts of the human mind, 14-15, 17, 19, 23, 24-25, 27, 30-31, 43-45, 47, 49-50, 62, 69-70, 84-85, 89-91, 92, 131
    contemporary discussions of, 22-25, 29-32, 51-56
    history of term, 18-22, 23
    relation to associationist psychology, 17, 25-29, 30, 35-36, 37-39, 41-43, 44-45, 107, 108-13, 124, 127, 128-31.
    views associated with contemporary, 22-23.
Jenks, Edward, *14*
Macaulay, Thomas Babington, *3, 33*
MacKenzie, James, 105
Mill, Harriet Taylor. *See* Taylor, Harriet
Mill, James:
    and John Stuart Mill's education, 2, 4, 5, 9, 10, 41-42, 88, 100-1, 114
    on government, 12-14
    on psychology, 11, 15, 17, 18, 26, 28-29, 31, *32*, 41-44, 45, 48,

61, 64-66, 69-70, 74, 76, 77, 80, 81, 83, *90*, 94, 100-1, 114-16
Mill, John Stuart:
    on art: and kinds of minds, 63-68, 73-75; narrative, 64-68, 72, 109; poetic, 48-49, 52, 60, 63-64, 68, 71-74, 75, 76, 78-79, 85, 89, 90, 91-92, 117-20, 121-22
    on associationist accounts of mental phenomena: and Benthamite utilitarianism, 28-29, 30, 33-38, 44-45, 46, 103; components of complex mental states, 41-42, 43-44, 64, 67, 69-71, 72-73, 76-77, 78-79, 80-81, 84, 92-94, 95-96, 101, 111-12, 115-16, 118-19, 121-24, 128-30; and consequentialism, 33-38, 67-68, 74-77, 92-93, 94-95; dissolution of complex mental states into component parts, 41-42, 43-44, 47, 69-70, 75-77; dominant feelings, 71, 79; dominant thoughts, 67-68, 69-71, 79; habitual associations, 17, 41-42, 43-48, 52-53, 59, 60, 64-65, 71-76, 89, 90, 91, 94-95, 96, 118-19, 121, 123; indissoluble associations, 70-71, 72-73, 75-77, 78-79, 84, 89-90, 92, 123; and introspection, 67, 76-77, 81-83, 85, 114, *116*; mental chemistry, 80-81, 84-85, 117-18, 120, 121, 126;

Index   135

mental mechanism, 114-15, 116-17; modifications to, 38-39, 50-51, 61-62, 63, 69-70, 74-77, 82-85, 97-100, 113, 116-17, 126; motivating associations, 26-29, 41-43, 46, 59-60, 61, 66-68, 69-70, 71-74, 78-80, 82-84, 88-89, 91, 95-96; natural associations, 45-46, 51, 53, 64, 89-92, *90*, 93-94, 111, 121-22; organic or physical associations, 45-46, 53, *90*; pleasure and pain, 26-29, 41-43, 80-84, 97-100, 127-28; principles governing association of ideas and impressions, 64-66, 76-78, 93-96, 98; problems with account of motivation, 61-62, 68-69, 87, 93-94

on Byron, Alfred Lord, 52, *52*, 60, 68, 72, 76, 90

on character: customary, 56-57, 61-62, 74, 113-15, 124, 126, 128, 129-30; national, *37*, *58*, *67*, 67, 68, 83; taxonomy of types, 56-60, 62, 63, *63*, 64-73, 74, 110, 115, 121-22, 123, 126; and will, 50-51, 59, 75-77, 112-13, 121-24, 126

childhood and early education, 2, 4, 41-42, 100-1, 114

on Coleridge, Samuel Taylor, 84-85

collaboration with Harriet Taylor, *3*, 8, 10, *10*, *13*, 104

contributions to psychology, 37-

39, 50-51, 61-62, 69-70, 74-77, 97-100, 113, 116-17, 126

on custom, 56-57, 61-62, 104, 111, 113-15, 124, 126, 128, 129-30

employment at East India House, 1, 2, 3-4, 6-7, 8-9, *12-13*, *62*

feminist influence of, *11-12*, *14*

first mental crisis: and employment at East India House, 4, 6-7; onset of, 41-43, 47-48, 116-17; possible causes of, *7*, 9, 42, *49*; recovery from, 48-49, 59-60, 74-76, 78-80, 84-85, 87-89, 91-92, 98-100, 101, 118-20, 122-23

gender-based criticism of, 11-15, 97

on higher and lower pleasures, 80-84, 115-16, 117-19, 124, 125

on introspective analysis, 67, 76-77, 81-83, 85, 114

Parliamentary ambitions and term of office, 2, 3, 7, 8, 14, 125

second mental crisis, 6, 8-9, *60*

on Wordsworth, William, 48-49, 51-53, 60, 71-74, 75, 76, 78-79, 85, 89, 90, 91-92, 118-120, 122

Millgram, Elijah, 23, 24, *32*, *47*

mind:

bifurcated accounts of, 11-12, 14-15, 17, 19, 23-29, 30-31, 43, 44-48, 62, 69-70, 73, 77, 80-84, 90-97, 100-1, 128-31

introspective analysis of, 67, 76-77, 81-83, 85, 114

laws governing association of ideas
and impressions, 64-66, 76-
78, 93-96, 98
moral psychology:
Benthamite, 11, 15, 17, 26-29,
32, 33-36, 37-38, 39, 41-44,
45, 46, 48, 61, 64-66, 67-68,
74, 76, 77, 83, 93-94, 96,
97, 100-1, 113-15
classical British, 25-29, 92-95
contemporary instrumentalist,
23-27, 29-30, 31-32, 46, 51-
57
Packe, Michael St. John, *5*
practical reason, general description of,
14-15
Quine, W. V. O., *100*
Quinn, Warren, 25, 30, 32
Railton, Peter, 51-56, 57, 59
Richardson, Henry, 50
Roebuck, John, *3*
Romilly, Samuel, *3*
Russell, Bertrand, 10-11, 13, 14, 15,
17, 19
Sappho, 82
Skorupski, John, 9
Stephen, Sir Leslie, 12-14, 17, 31, *42*,
45
Stillinger, Jack, *3*, *10*
Stokes, Eric, *13*
Strutt, Edward, *3*
Taylor, Harriet:
collaboration with John Stuart
Mill, *3*, 8, 10, *13*, 104
early ambition, 4-8
influence on John Stuart Mill, 6,
7, 8, 9, 10-11, 104
and John Stuart Mill's
Autobiography, 3, *3*, 6, 7-8, 9

and *On Liberty*, *10*, 104
relationship with John Stuart Mill,
3-6, 7-9, 10, 11-12, *13*, 14,
104
Taylor, John, 3, 4, 5-6
Thornton, W. T., *1*
Tooke, Eyton, *3*
utilitarianism:
anti-consequentialist, 36-39, 103
Benthamite consequentialist, 26-
29, 35-38, 103
and higher pleasures, 103
and instrumentalism about practical reason, 26-29
utility. *See* happiness
Villiers, Charles, *3*
Wilson, Fred, *26*, 76-77, *81*
Wilson, John, *104*
Wundt, Wilhelm, 27
Zastoupil, Lynn, *13*